FASTEN YOUR SEATBELT: THE PASSENGER IS FLYING THE PLANE

Dedicated to the memory of my mother, Shanti Devi,
for her unconditional love, kindness and support

Fasten Your Seatbelt:
The Passenger is Flying the Plane

NAWAL K. TANEJA

ASHGATE

Published by
Ashgate Publishing Limited
Gower House
Croft Road
Aldershot
Hampshire GU11 3HR
England

Ashgate Publishing Company
Suite 420
101 Cherry Street
Burlington, VT 05401-4405
USA

Ashgate website: http://www.ashgate.com

British Library Cataloguing in Publication Data
Taneja, Nawal, K.
   Fasten your seatbelt: the passenger is flying the plane
   1.Airlines - Management 2.Consumer behavior 3.Airlines -
   Finance
   I.Title
   387.7'068

Library of Congress Cataloging-in-Publication Data
Taneja, Nawal, K.
   Fasten your seatbelt : the passenger is flying the plane / by Nawal K. Taneja.
        p. cm.
   Includes index.
        ISBN 0-7546-4528-2
   1. Airlines. 2. Airlines--Customer services. 3. Airlines--Rates. 4. Consumer
behavior. 5. Consumers' preferences. 6. Consumer satisfaction. I. Title.
   HE9776.T362 2005
   387.7'068'8--dc22

                                                                          2005014424

ISBN 0 7546 4528 2

Printed and bound in Great Britain by MPG Books Ltd, Bodmin, Cornwall

Contents

List of Figures

List of Tables

Foreword

Bill Brunger
Senior Vice President
Network
Continental Airlines

The Airline Industry is changing at an accelerating pace. In the pages that follow, Nawal Taneja will make this point convincingly. The major enabler of the change has been the Internet, which has been revolutionary for two primary reasons: It has created a direct link between the customer and the airline, and it has facilitated the emergence and initial success of a new crop of apparently viable new entrants. Using the Internet, the passenger has direct, transparent, un-intermediated access to the complete range of alternative fares and services—really for the first time in history—and the airline can create a direct, personalized relationship with each customer. For the new entrant or "unconventional" carrier, the Internet, combined with eTicketing, has removed the largest barrier-to-entry into the business, by solving the ticket delivery/distribution problem.

A change this fundamental requires everyone, consumers, incumbent airlines, new-entrants, and potential competitors, to think and rethink deeply about their plans. In *Fasten Your Seatbelt: The Passenger is Flying the Plane*, Nawal Taneja masterfully lays out the issues and describes many of the new products and business models that must come forward, both real and on-the-drawing-board. Not all new ideas will flourish—the marketplace will judge the effectiveness of airlines-within-airlines (Song, Ted, and the like), premium products (UA.ps, "more legroom in coach"), pillowless-ness, "rolling hubs", really big airplanes, fractional jets, mergers between weak entities, and all of the other concepts designed to counter the chaos. For all participants, Taneja notes, this is a time for careful thought.

We at Continental continue to believe that thoughtful adaptation and nimble adjustment, rather than radical surgery, will drive future success. To me, the key to understanding the future may be Figure 4.10 in this book. It is useful to note that the absolute size of the Revenue/RASM premium enjoyed by legacy carriers has *not* diminished over time. If the cost curve for the legacy carriers had followed the same trajectory as that of the "unconventionals", then both groups would currently be experiencing similar profits. It is the CASM differential that has grown—largely because it has been harder for large incumbents to react quickly and flexibly to the marketplace trauma of the "perfect storm" of September 11, the economic downturn and soaring fuel prices. Labor cost issues are currently being worked at the negotiating table—hopefully in structurally permanent ways by which employees and shareholders share upside in good times, and bear, together, the effects of down-cycles.

With media attention focused on the cost side of the equation, the resilience of legacy carriers' RASM is often overlooked. While it is always important to reexamine all entrenched business practices, the RASM results indicate that full hub-and-spoke networks provide insulation by allowing legacy carriers to build load factors; that premium cabins can continue to attract full fare customers; that sophisticated revenue management systems focus appropriately on higher-yield markets and segments; that multiple fleet types can be used to tailor capacity to demand; and that a breadth of geographical offerings can allow nimble carriers to migrate assets toward better opportunities. In all these areas, legacy carriers have substantive advantages. Granted there is work to be done, but there is still a lot of value in this "Old Model".

And unconventional airlines still have plenty of thinking to do. UltrAir, AirOne, MGMGrand, and other defunct "high service" carriers are evidence that monotone focus on a market niche may not work, and PeopleExpress, Braniff I, II and III, and Continental's own abortive ContinentaLite experiment, among others, serve as a reminder that you can build an airline so cheap that no one wants to fly on it. No one is immune from the need to continuously rethink (a point Nawal Taneja makes repeatedly). The new crop is no exception.

Darwin pertains here—*most* experiments, and *all* of the dinosaurs that do not adapt will fail. They will fail most quickly and spectacularly if they ignore the customer. The only alternative is to evolve.

Nawal Taneja will guide you through the issues, describe where things stand and provoke your thinking. Read on.

Houston, Texas
June 2005

Foreword

John Elkins
Executive Vice President
Brand, Marketing, and Corporate Relations
VISA International

When an industry goes through fundamental structural change, it should be no surprise that experts in the field call for an overhaul of the business model and a review of the customer value proposition. The global airline industry is well into such a dramatic change and more forecasts of the demise of the incumbents provide little practical value. Insights into innovative solutions and the identification of new market opportunities however are a rarer offering and a different matter.

In my experience working with industries experiencing such change, especially regulated industries like financial services, telecommunications and energy, structural change requires structural answers. Entrenched management is rarely capable of making the necessary tradeoffs and necessary overhauls. Bringing management from other industries can help, but the fundamental requirement is big doses of innovation and growth. Most industry veterans facing down the twin challenges of customer disaffection and new entrants, try saving their way to the future. It is almost always a flawed strategy.

As with the airline industry many of the regulated sectors that I have mentioned, including others like health care and pharmaceuticals, experienced significant over-capacity at precisely the moment that new entrants appeared, in part fueling customer disaffection. There is many a disappointed investor that has bought into the well versed "consolidation" story. This is usually the first bastion of retreat and few succeed—known by many in business as "dinosaurs mating."

The fact of the matter is that there has been a fundamental shift taking place whereby the power in the airline industry value chain has moved in proportion to the value of the assets. Property, plant and equipment were major barriers to entry at the outset of the "hub and spoke" era. Today they have become liabilities as knowledge and technology have put power at the disposal of consumers and Global Distribution Systems. Intangibles like brand and IP have taken over the industry power arrangements and turned the economics upside down.

In his new book *Fasten Your Seatbelt: The Passenger is Flying the Plane* Nawal Taneja addresses some of the airlines' woes with his "Birds Eye" view of the landscape focusing on what is shaping the airline and travel industry. An objective analyst and an active advisor for many years within the aviation industry, Taneja looks both inside and out for solutions to these structural problems.

He starts where all good change agents look first, at the consumer. He examines how the interests and needs of various consumers are best being served and recognized and reevaluates their behavior. The new segmentation is eye opening. His analysis looks at changing what already exists in the industry as well as bringing in ideas from the outside.

Taneja also introduces the importance of alliances and partnerships. When industries go through structural change this is often the difference between surviving and thriving. It enables traditional players to exchange core competencies and important equities. The lines delineating the distinction between travel, transport, entertainment and information are blurring, the response by management must include a willingness to reach out and partner in new and different ways. If the right partnerships are chosen incumbents get the added benefit of specialization and speed, essential ingredients in fostering change.

Industry sectors with large capital and fixed asset requirements and embedded infrastructure are always vulnerable to change. The airline industry seems to be a habitual victim. It is probably time to think of even bigger structural reform. The time has come to consider the need for part of the industry to be a "utility" based transport system supported by governments, while the other part is a free market, entrepreneurially managed and financed one. The telecommunications industry is fast approaching this model.

While Taneja doesn't go quite this far in this book, his insights are practical and instructive in moving the "change agenda" forward for the airline industry.

San Francisco, California
June 1, 2005

Foreword

Samuel L. Katz
Chairman and Chief Executive Officer
Travel Distribution Services
Cendant Corporation

Low-cost carriers have forever altered the competitive landscape by proving collaborative work rules, no-frills (or value driven) service, and employee-shared success create a sustainable and profitable model that benefits employees, airlines, shareholders and most of all, customers. Airlines are not alone in having to deal with the forces of change and competition.

For example, the traditional travel distribution model was once centered solely around the Global Distribution System (GDS) computer reservation platforms with one size fits all services and pricing for airlines and agencies. Now, the airline, which is the intermediary's customer, is *"Flying the Plane"*. At Cendant Travel Distribution Services, we are committed to an exciting future of travel distribution which extends well beyond the GDS and, as such, we have been focused on offering our airline customers the value of an integrated travel distribution model which delivers a compelling portfolio, helping airlines increase sales volume through multiple channels with the benefit of both price transparency and opacity for a total lower cost.

The question one should continue to ask is – which carriers will emerge as winners and leaders in this marketplace? While opinions will, no doubt, vary, consensus is likely to point to those carriers that have abandoned the legacy airline model and taken the bold steps to adopt a more sustainable and cooperative model to cut costs and increase distribution in innovative ways. Airlines must be active participants in changing the old paradigm with customers and business partners alike. And, those airlines who fail to engage will be more challenged than ever as they may be more interested in legacy thinking around market control rather than a focus on increasing sales and lowering costs.

Cendant knows the value of transforming its distribution model to better serve its customer base in a manner unrivaled in the industry. Like the newer generation of airlines who are providing greater value, our strategy is simple, but effective: build volume and reduce costs so that all participants in the distribution chain can be successful.

Fasten Your Seatbelt: The Passenger is Flying the Plane not only helps to define what are the driving forces in the industry overall that are influencing the demise of the traditional airlines as we know it (or forcing them to reinvent themselves), but what to expect moving forward. Fasten your seat belt; it's a going to be an exciting future.

Parsippany, New Jersey
June 6, 2005

Foreword

Stefan H. Lauer
Member of the Executive Board
Lufthansa German Airlines

'Globalizer' vs. 'Localizer'

Struck by a series of successive crises and external shocks the aviation industry entered a state of disorder at the beginning of this century. The successful business model of the network carriers proved to be extremely vulnerable to external effects like September 11th, the Iraq war, and SARS. The leading airlines unexpectedly had to cope with less demand, more competition, lower yields and an inflexible high cost base. Huge losses at major airlines were the consequence. The process of industry consolidation accelerated and opportunities opened up for new players.

At the same time the business model of the low cost, point-to-point carriers seemed to be only little, if at all, affected by the external influences which caused the major crisis for the traditional network carriers. It seemed that this business model was superior to the business model of the traditional network carriers. Consequently a multitude of new carriers and spin-offs appeared all over the world, eager to copy the low cost, point-to-point business model.

The consolidation process of the traditional network carriers together with the growing number of point-to-point low cost carriers have resulted in an open competition for the most successful business model. While the traditional carriers targeted airline customers with a broad network and differentiated services, the low cost carriers offered them rock-bottom prices. It appeared to be a battle for an all-dominant business model, the model of the 'Globalizer' versus the model of the 'Localizer'.

Today experience tells us two things:

Firstly, both business models have their advantages and limitations. Therefore, neither model is superior to the other. For example, most industry experts underestimated the growth potential of the Localizers. At the beginning of this century only a handful of Localizers operated in Europe with a total market share of less than five percent. It was widely believed that the European network carriers learned their lessons and could set the entry barriers high enough to prevent those new entrants from entering their markets. Today the European market counts dozens of Localizers with a combined and continuously growing market share of already twenty percent! Nonetheless, the business model of the Localizer has not always proved to be successful. Several of those new found companies have already gone out of business. More are expected to follow. Furthermore, only a few of today's Localizers operate profitably. Also, the Localizers' business model cannot serve the needs of the global traveler, where connectivity and network play a decisive role.

Secondly, there is no longer a clear difference between the business model of the Globalizer and the model of the Localizer. Both started to change their business model towards each other and the formerly distinctive characteristics have become partly blurred. Globalizers started to match the Localizers price levels, reduce service levels, cut their cost base, and extend their point-to-point routes. Simultaneously, Localizers started to increase their service levels with the introduction of loyalty programs, free of charge in-flight entertainment, and in some cases, even catering. Moreover, Localizers started to build network structures, 'hubbing by coincidence' transformed to planned hubbing, including code-sharing and baggage transfers. Customers, business travelers and private travelers, are now taking advantage of both business models.

So there is no longer a battle for the predominant business model. Certainly, the transformation process is still ongoing and airlines still experiment with different parts of both models. But it is now evident that these experiments are necessary and will ultimately lead to new forms of viable business models which will combine the most successful elements of the Globalizer and the Localizer model.

In his new book *Fasten Your Seatbelt* Nawal Taneja again manages to deliver a very detailed and revealing insight into today's airline industry. His deep comprehension and knowledge of our industry delivers a very profound analysis of the problems we are facing and the tasks we have to accomplish. The book outstandingly illustrates the transition phase of our industry and gives useful guidelines on how to adapt towards the design of a viable, clearly customer oriented business model.

Frankfurt, Germany
June 2005

Foreword

Andrew Lobbenberg
European Airline Equity Research
ABN AMRO Bank

The economics of the airline industry defy gravity with more aplomb than the A380. Airlines are serial value destroyers and yet they continue somehow to attract capital. Investors can make good returns putting money into airlines, but they need great timing and stupendous luck.

The most obvious way to build a successful airline would be to start from scratch as the unconventional airlines illustrate. Yet a clean sheet of paper is not an option for established airlines. The operating environment is not going to get easier. Both US and European airlines are diverting capacity from short haul markets, ravaged by Southwest, easyJet and the like, to long haul routes, which currently produce superior profits. The excess capacity and sick economics of short haul markets are being exported. Start up carriers, today from the Gulf, but in the future from India and China too, are also going to invade today's profitable long haul markets with frightening levels of capacity and daunting cost advantages. Moreover, liberalisation will ultimately erode margins in those rare but extremely important supra-normal profit markets that exist as a result of enduring regulatory constraints.

What now? The airline industry is not short of intellectual horsepower focused on it. There are many very bright people in airline senior management working for far less than they could earn in healthier industries. Equally there is a plethora of overpaid though sometimes bright bankers and consultants focusing on the industry. But these brains lack objectivity. As with all of Nawal Taneja's writing, this book takes an independent, global and very thought-provoking view of the challenges of the industry.   Whilst there's no magic bullet solution Mr. Taneja has many insightful ideas.   Enjoy the book.

London, England
5th May, 2005

Foreword

Kyung Ha Ma
Vice President, Corporate Strategy and Planning
Asiana Airlines

Given that globalization is a fact, not just a trend, to succeed businesses must now identify new drivers of socio-economic power and growth on the one hand and the developments and adoptions of technology, on the other hand.

Consider, for example, the case of socio-economic characteristics. It is no longer sufficient just to consider the economic viability of countries as destinations. We must now consider regions. For example, the makeup of the population and the dynamic growth in Bangalore, India or Dalian, China are very different than the average for India and China, which are strategically important markets for carriers in South Korea.

Similarly, while it is important to try to look into the future of technology, it is even more important to try to look into the dynamics with which technology is likely to be adopted. Take the case of teleconferencing. While viable technology has been available for some time, it appears to have had minimal effect on business travel habits. However, the upcoming generation of business travelers, who are likely to have been raised on networked technologies, could adopt to those technologies differently—another dimension of customer focus.

Future business strategies of airlines will be shaped by not only the location of economic powers but also of the behaviour of consumers living within these economic centers. Mr. Taneja's new book, *Fasten Your Seatbelt: The Passenger is Flying the Plane* is valuable—relevant, timely, and conceptually sound—for airline corporate planners to focus on the current and future customers in the important global regions. He has amply demonstrated the power consumers have had in shaping the business strategies of airlines in North America and Europe. We must now examine the impact of this customer power not only within the Asia-Pacific region, but also in the emerging regions.

Mr. Taneja's discussion on fragmentation and segmentation within the customer-driven marketplace is particularly thought provoking. Traditional airlines now face ferocious competition not only from other traditional airlines but also from new entrants in the long haul intercontinental markets, for example the carriers based in the Middle East (as discussed by Mr. Taneja). Moreover, aircraft technology is now available to establish alternative network design to compete more effectively with all types of competitors and at the same time provide value for customers. The ultimate key, as the book states, is to develop business designs that provide value to the targeted segments of customers who in turn provide value to the airline to earn a reasonable return on investment for its shareholders.

Seoul, Korea
31 May, 2005

Foreword

Edward Nicol
Director Information Management and CIO
Cathay Pacific Airways

The aviation industry is in trouble: the marketplace is changing and customer segments are fragmenting. New entrants with lower costs and different, flexible and responsive business models are taking advantage of liberalisation and new market opportunities to outwit many established airlines with legacy costs, processes and mindsets.

Recent IATA annual general meetings have called for an industry-led simplification of the business and for governments to recognize the important role the industry plays and for them to bring their regulations and infrastructure into line with twenty-first century requirements.

Simplicity is not just "all good": there are trade-offs with flexibility and complexity. Nawal Taneja makes the point eloquently that customer needs are changing and are much more variable than recognised hitherto and need greater recognition. Meeting their needs is critical in any industry and aviation is no exception.

The airlines that will succeed are those that identify the customer segments they wish to serve and clearly understand their expectations and the product sets they value. Airlines need to be ruthless about creating and delivering only those products which meet their customers' needs and which they are prepared to pay for. These may be as complex or as simple as the marketplace dictates— a point made several times in *Fasten Your Seatbelt*. The next step though is to deliver these products as simply and cost-effectively as possible, discarding all surplus product elements and redundant processes.

Information Technology can play a huge role in this. Its practitioners can bring process and analysis to the identification and design stages and are responsible for much of the enablement and deployment. The keys to success are an IT team which has a record of success in delivery and the skills and opportunity to engage the business at all levels. Businesses are forever seeking to make IT strategic and here is the opportunity.

Aviation is going though a period of great change. The old business model is not just broken: it is dead. Aviation is a business though and the standard rules apply. Identify and know your customers, design and deliver products they value at prices they are prepared to pay and success will surely follow. The airlines that follow these rules will be the ones that succeed.

Hong Kong
10 June 2005

Foreword

Nicole W. Piasecki
Executive Vice President
Business Strategy and Marketing
Boeing Commercial Airplanes

As the airline industry has moved steadily from a highly regulated industry to an increasingly liberalized one, competition has intensified dramatically. In today's liberalized business environment, the markets, not the regulators, decide which airlines will succeed and which will fail. This ultimately means that today more than ever before, airlines are intensely focused on a fundamental question: What do passengers want? Successfully answering this question is the key to winning in the marketplace.

Accordingly, the commercial aviation environment is changing rapidly. A surge in innovation has significantly benefited the traveling public. The last several years have seen an explosion in innovative airline business models. Technological advancements have brought further innovations in airplanes, in the application of revenue management, and in the use of the Internet to streamline and simplify operations and transactions. Much of this effort is directed at attracting and pleasing passengers.

Productivity improvements continue to make safe, convenient and affordable air travel available to millions of new airline customers each year. As liberalization continues and air traffic increases, competition continues to escalate as well. Airlines are relentless in the pursuit of passengers, and determined to serve passenger choice in new and innovative ways. In fact, airlines have recently begun to use technology and business model innovation to exclusively target specific sub-segments of the passenger customer base.

How will these efforts change and shape our industry?

Nawal Taneja's extensive study *Fasten Your Seatbelt: The Passenger is Flying the Plane* explores this question. Taneja examines possibilities in pricing, scheduling, networks, distribution and other key areas of the business to identify trends that are transforming commercial aviation. The result is an illuminating and provocative look at where our industry is today and where it will be tomorrow. This is vital information for those of us who work in the industry. Given the many businesses with significant ties to commercial air travel, coupled with the substantial role the industry plays in the global economy, Taneja's work will be of great interest to the rest of the world as well.

Seattle, Washington
June 2, 2005

Preface

Fasten Your Seatbelt: The Passenger is Flying the Plane is the fourth book in a series written at the encouragement of practitioners who are suggesting that structural change in the global airline industry be discussed further. Its central theme is that core customers—not airline management—are beginning to seize control of the direction of the industry.[1] In July 2004 IATA met in Singapore for its Annual General Meeting in an atmosphere of on-going crisis, including the Iraq War, the impact of SARS, and sharply escalating oil prices. Airline executives came to the meeting, some struggling with bankruptcy protection, some near bankruptcy and others concerned about the huge expected losses. They had renegotiated labor agreements, cancelled or delayed aircraft deliveries, changed the structure of their networks and fleet and forged new supplier relationships. By any standards these wrenching changes did not appear to accomplish nearly enough for the long term.

Unfortunately—despite the efforts of some intelligent, well-meaning, and hard-working executive teams—the inescapable conclusion remains that a large segment of the industry is still in crisis and seems incapable of lifting itself out on a sustained basis. In his speech, the Director General and the CEO of IATA echoed the message of my last book, *Simpli-Flying*, stating "consumers pay for value, not for complexity", and suggested an agenda to "simplify the business".[2] Although airlines have been simplifying their operations, products, and pricing structures, the global airline industry that lost almost $5 billion in 2004 is expected to lose about $6 billion in 2005.[3] Although high fuel prices certainly contribute to the losses, the root cause appears to be the continuing negative gap between revenue yield and costs for traditional airlines, compared to the positive gap for newer generation airlines. This situation implies that customers are taking their business to the newer generation of airlines who, presumably, are providing greater value.

Fasten Your Seatbelt suggests that past strategies have, at best, enabled some traditional airlines to survive, some to have developed staying power, but very few to achieve sustainable profits. Unfortunately, the marketplace is going to become even more competitive, not only because of the expansion of new generation airlines but also because of the expansion of new major network airlines—such as those based in the Middle East—as well as new players (expansion of organizations offering fractional ownership in corporate jets and the viability of on demand air taxis). At the same time, customer expectations are escalating, resulting in increasing dissatisfaction with the price-service options and customer processes of many traditional airlines.

This book deals with the changing realities of the aviation marketplace in three parts.

- The first part—Chapters 1 and 2—is about (a) the changing behavior of customers in general and the changing expectations and mix of airline passengers, and (b) the initiatives managements have taken, what has worked and what has not.
- Having taken into consideration the evolving consumer concerns and the turbulence in the marketplace, the second part—Chapters 3 through 7—discusses the need to break from the past and to undertake a meaningful redesign of the overall business based on customer segmentation, followed by management of customers as financial investments.
- The third part—Chapter 8—argues that if the whole issue relates more to value than price, what does airline management need to do to transform their companies to produce and deliver value?

While the message in *Fasten Your Seatbelt* is mainly targeted at traditional network airlines—to survive, they must transform the business swiftly and dramatically by thinking differently—new generation airlines do not get a free ride either. They must not allow their initial success to lead to arrogance. In addition to cost increases from a maturing workforce and fleet, they face the next generation of airlines ready to exploit technology and new generation aircraft to implement even more value delivering business models.

The main audience continues to be senior level practitioners of all segments within the global airline industry, including the traditional or legacy network airlines (henceforth referred to as conventional airlines) and the low-cost, low fare and low complexity airlines (henceforth called unconventional airlines). And, as with the earlier books, the approach is still to provide impartial, candid and pragmatic analyses based on *what is happening in the actual marketplace.*

Notes

[1]   The first, *Driving Airline Business Strategies through Emerging Technology* showed that in the rapidly evolving airline industry, emerging technologies could indeed play an increasingly critical role in the delivery of real and perceived customer value. The second, *Airline Survival Kit*, wrestled with the precipitous decline in the profitability of the industry and discussed some strategies for dealing with the heavy burden of excessive complexity incorporated within the operations of legacy airlines. Having realized that the industry and the environment was changed forever, the third, *Simpli-Flying*, drilled deeper into the discussion on restructuring of markets and the critical need for strategies to adjust to the new aviation realities

[2]   Bisignani, Giovanni, *State of the Air Transport Industry*, A Report by the Director General and CEO of the International Air Transport Association at the World Air Transport Summit, 60th Annual General Meeting, Singapore, June 7, 2004.

[3]   "Air-Travel Industry Says Governments Need to Lower Taxes", *Wall Street Journal*, May 31, 2005, p. D4.

Acknowledgements

I would like to express my appreciation for all those who made this book possible, especially the Executive Editor, Jim Hunt (formerly with Air Canada) and the Contributing Editor, Jim Oppermann (formerly with America West) and: ABA Air Business Academy—Paul Clark; ABN Amro Bank—Andrew Lobbenberg; Aer Lingus—Paul Brady, and Brian Dunne; Airbus—David Jones; Air New Zealand—Ralph Norris and Paul Skellon; Air Transport Association—John Heimlich; Air Transport World—Geoffrey Thomas; Alaska Airlines—Don Garvett and Robert Reeder; All Nippon Airways—Masashi Izumi and Tadashi Matsushita; Amadeus—Stephane Pingaud and Peter von Moltke; American Airlines—Scott Nason; Boeing—Cian Dooley, John Feren and Kent Fisher; Bombardier Aerospace—Chuck Evans and Warren Hoppe; British Airways—Andrew Sentance and William Walsh; Business Travel Coalition—Kevin Mitchell; Cathay Pacific—Edward Nicol; Cendant—Flo Lugli; Centre of Asia Pacific Aviation—Andrew Miller; Continental Airlines—William Brunger, Robert Cortelyou, John Slater and James Stevens; Cranfield University—Fariba Alamdari; Ford Motor Company—Matt Taneja; General Electric Aircraft Engines—Lorraine Bolsinger, Bill Brown and Gary Leonard; Hawaiian Airlines—Mark Dunkerley and Richard Peterson; Informative—Brad Ferguson; Insideout-C2C—Bonnie Reitz (formerly with Continental Airlines); Limited Brands—Lisa MacCartney; Lufthansa Airlines—Olaf Backofen, Holger Hätty and Dietmar Kirchner; McKinsey Company—Lucio Pompeo; NetJets—Rachael Estepp and Richard Smith; Online Travel Review—Jared Blank; Outrigger Hotels and Resorts—Robert Solomon and Perry Sorenson; Qantas—David Cox; SAS—Axel Blom, Jan Lundborg, Finn Thaulow and Teddy Zebitz; Shell International—Peter Cornelius; Singapore Airlines—Stanley Kuppusamy and Subhas Menon; Southwest Airlines—Adam Decaire, Michael Friedman, John Jamotta, Kevin Krone, Pete McGlade and Todd Newcomer; Summus—Eva Schmatz; TACA—Alfredo Schildknecht;

Teradata of NCR—Steve Dworkin, Brendan Hickman and Peeter A. Kivestu; Trevelyan Associates—Robert Trevelyan; Unisys—Steve Arsenault, Cynthia Crowley, Olivier Houri and Michael McNamara; US Department of Transportation—Randy Bennett and Todd Homan; Virgin Atlantic—Sheila Ellis, Sian Foster, and Barry Humphreys; and VISA International—Deborah Arnold, John Elkins, Karen Gullett, Tom Shepard and Sonia Reed.

There are a number of other people who provided significant help: at the Ohio State University—research (Dr. Chul Lee), exhibits (Nick LaRusso and Sam Vinci); the production of the book at the Ashgate Publishing Company (Guy Loft—Commissioning Editor, Pauline Beavers—Desk Editor and Adrian Shanks—Marketing Manager). Finally, I would like to thank my family, for their support and patience.

List of Abbreviations

ASM	Available Seat Miles
CASM	Cost per Available Seat Mile
CRM	Customer Relationship Management
FFP	Frequent Flyer Programs
GDSs	Global Distribution Systems
HDTV	High Definition Television
JFK	New York, JFK Airport
LHR	London Heathrow Airport
O&D	Origin and Destination
RASM	Revenue per Available Seat Mile
RPM	Revenue Passenger Miles
SARS	Severe Acute Respiratory Syndrome
SIFL	Standard Industry Fare Level
ULH	Ultra Long Haul
VFR	Visiting Friends and Relatives
VLJ	Very Light Jets
3XX	The 300 Series of Airbus Aircraft, including the 300, 310, 318, 319, 320, 321, 330, 340, 350 and 380
7YY	The 700 Series of Boeing Aircraft, including the 717, 727, 737, 747, 757, 767, 777 and 787

List of Abbreviations

Chapter 1

Introducing the New Pilots

In the early years of commercial aviation, the "golden age" of air travel, real pilots ran the airline industry, bringing the romance of flight to the select group of passengers who could afford to fly. In the post deregulation era, airline CEOs emerged from other industries to pilot the airlines into the future. Since 2000, though, many US major airlines have lost their CEOs, and the passengers have abandoned traditional airlines en masse. Airlines must now come to terms with the fact that, in the commercial sense, the passenger is flying the plane.

These pilots are the passengers who have grown less and less satisfied with the services provided by conventional airlines but who have had no other options. However, within the last few years, other options developed quickly. With the exception of one or two airlines, the first generation of new airlines achieved low costs (through, for example, the use of very old airplanes and poor services) to provide low fares, but not necessarily good value. Though unhappy, passengers stayed with the conventional airlines. Then came a new generation of airlines—henceforth called unconventional airlines—who offered not just lower fares but much better value, derived from different business models (new aircraft, comfortable seats, state-of-the-art in-flight entertainment, friendly service, and so forth). As a result, passengers now have options and core customers—not airline management—are beginning to seize control of the direction of the industry.

The airline industry is going through a sea of change as a result of the confluence of three major forces:

- the expansion of acceptable services provided by unconventional airlines,

- the proliferation of the use of the Internet, and

- the economic stresses on all businesses (resulting from the economic slowdown coupled with events such as September 11, 2001, SARS, and the Iraq War).

Our passengers—"the new pilots"—have quickly embraced the new price-service options resulting from the changing dynamics within the airline industry.

This chapter starts with highlights of some broad customer behavior trends and follows that with their implications to the airline industry. With changes in the make up of economies, consumer demographics and technology, the customer base has become increasingly less homogeneous. Although there continue to be business, leisure and VFR travelers, as exemplified below, there are numerous sub-categories between each of the three major categories. This chapter will discuss the economic stresses felt by these consumers and the ramifications of theses stresses on the airline industry.

Summarizing Customer Behavior Trends

Dozens of excellent books have been written on customer and business trends and their impact on customer strategies. The following list provides a summary of some key customer trends to whet the appetite of the reader for further insights into the fundamental areas of change in consumer behavior.

- Power is shifting from businesses to consumers. Consequently, if businesses want to succeed, they must offer a value adding selling proposition. Similarly, this shift in power is leading to increasing amounts of disintermediation.[1]

- Customers are busy people who are forced to deal with voluminous correspondence—emails, voice mail, and so forth.[2] The last thing they need is more meaningless communications from businesses pushing their products and services.

- Customers not only have greater demands, but they also want their demands to be heard, that is to say, customers are no longer "passive". They want to be engaged.

- Customers want quality products and reliable services.

- Customers want fair value for money. They are no longer willing to pay for a bundle of irrelevant features.

- Customers' expectations are escalating and the failure to meet these expectations has meant a decline in their satisfaction ratings.[3]

- Customers are now much more discerning.

- Customers want products and services rapidly, and they want to be able to multi-task, for example, watch television and work on the computer at the same time.

- Customers are willing to pay a premium for emotionally important goods and services that deliver the perceived value of quality. Consider, for example, people looking for experience when they go out to eat in a restaurant or look for books at Barnes and Noble.

- Customers want choice—a broader range of goods and services.

- Customers want brand name products but they want them at lower prices.

- Customers want "deals", more than the "dealer".

- Customers want to "take care of themselves, look after number one, reward themselves, and build their self-esteem".[4]

- Nowadays, loyalty has become a casualty of changing consumer culture. People simply want more and better goods at prices they consider "reasonable".[5]

- Consumers are reluctant to trust the information provided by businesses. Instead, they turn to sources that they trust—independent third party organizations, personal contacts, and so forth.

These characteristics of consumer behavior are the result of a confluence and alignment of numerous social, economic, technical, and business factors, including:

- Mass discount retailers which for many years have been reducing their costs and compressing their margins (through flexible supply chains and global re-sourcing), are making goods and services available to an increasing portion of the middle class.[6]

- Large low-cost retailers are now stocking much larger selections and brand named goods that they offer for sale at everyday low prices.

- More people are under increasing amounts of stress relating to jobs, family life, and now, more recently, travel.

- The Internet is giving consumers greater consumer knowledge and insight into pricing behavior. The web has facilitated the search for, and a validation of, consumer sought information.

- During the past 50 years, there has been a continuous growth in the availability of "convenience" goods and services.

- Globalization of business and trade is increasing the selection of goods and services available to consumers.

- There has been a steep change in demographic and cultural shifts. Around the world (Brazil, China, India, Russia, and so forth) there has been an increase in household wealth over the past two decades. This increase in wealth is partly the result of an increase in incomes, partly due to an increase in the value of peoples' homes, partly due to an increase in education levels and partly due to (in the case of India and China) huge exporting of manufacturing and call center jobs.

- Consumers are now better traveled (for example, due to better services and lower fares), having acquired a good knowledge of tastes and styles from foreign destinations.

- The media has become a strong and instant communicator of information worldwide.

- Technology is changing rapidly—a trend that, in turn, is changing social norms.

- In some regions of the world there is a fusion of cultures as communications spread and boundaries blur between countries.[7] In other regions, tensions are increasing due to a clash of cultures.

- In the US, there has been a significant reduction in the number of traditional families. Less than one quarter of American households contain a married couple with children living at home. Consequently, there are more "singles" with more money to spend on themselves.[8]

- People are living longer and older people have new opportunities available to them.

- The status of women continues to evolve. They are playing an increasing role—in the workforce, as consumers and as influencers.

- Mismanagement of brand name products and businesses— Vioxx and Enron—has cost consumer confidence.

Decreasing Homogeneity of the Airline Customer Base

Consider the confluence of two trends. First, many industries, airlines included, have remained much more product than customer focused. Second, as shown by the examples below, the airline customer base has become increasingly less homogenous. The increase in heterogeneity of the passenger traffic flows has not started to show up in typical conventional airline network strategies or other areas of marketing—websites, call centers and so forth. Consider the following hypothetical examples of business, leisure and VFR travelers and think about the value gaps between passengers' expectations and airlines' offerings.

The New Business Travelers

The New Hampshire Netjetter

- Fifty-two year old Chief Financial Officer of an Investment Conglomerate with subsidiaries all over the United States.
- Nationwide business trips average twice a week.
- Makes $8 million a year (a compensation that has doubled over past 10 years).
- Used to fly first class on conventional airlines out of Manchester, New Hampshire, almost always via hub-and-spoke systems.

- "Burned" accrued miles for vacations in Florida and Europe.
- Switched to NetJets subscription after 2001: saving enormously on travel times; most business trips are now for one day, requiring no overnight stays; typical gain on travel time averages 6 hours per roundtrip; used to pay an average of $2,500 per trip, now pays $6,000 resulting in cost of $600 per hour saved.
- Now still vacations in Florida, but flies for pleasure/VFR on JetBlue.
- Buys travel through an assistant for business travel and on the Internet for private travel.

The London City Business Banker

- Forty-nine year old Investment Banker in a large British bank doing business in New York and Continental Europe.
- Two trips to the United States per month, one European trip per week.
- Makes £300,000 a year (lost most of the bonus payments after 2000).
- Used to fly Concorde to New York (and back overnight in first class on wide body aircraft) and business class throughout Europe.
- "Burned" accrued miles on British Airways for family holidays in the Caribbean and South Africa.
- After a cost cutting initiative, the bank switched to business roundtrips purchased in New York to avoid the overpriced market in London.
- Trips within Europe are now made in the economy class and on easyJet whenever possible.
- Uses miles to get first class upgrades on eastbound trans-Atlantic flights.
- Buys tickets for business on the company intranet travel site.

The Silicon Valley Coach Consultant

- Thirty-four year old MBA working for small IT consulting firm in Palo Alto.
- Makes one domestic roundtrip per week.
- Makes $110,000 a year (down from $225,000 in 2000).
- Used to fly business class, mostly on United out of San Francisco.
- "Burned" accrued miles on United for vacations in Hawaii.
- After avoiding bankruptcy, the company switched to Southwest flights out of San Jose.
- Now uses Southwest bonus miles for weekend trips to Las Vegas and Phoenix.
- Buys tickets on Southwest's website.

The DaimlerChrysler Detroit Shuttler

- Fifty-six year old power train engineer from Stuttgart, working on a company-wide standardization project.
- Makes three roundtrips to Auburn Hills each month.
- Makes €180,000 a year (20 percent over 2000).
- Used to fly Lufthansa via Frankfurt and Detroit in business class.
- "Burned" accrued miles on Lufthansa on flights to his condominium in Majorca.
- Now uses company shuttle service (the 319).
- Holds annual pass for Majorca flights on LTU.
- Does not have to buy tickets.

The Bangalore BPO Entrepreneur

- Forty-three year old, with British MBA degree, founded a BPO company for CRM adoption software.
- Makes two round trips to the United States, one to Europe and one to Australia every month.
- Makes $60,000 a year (made almost nothing 5 years ago).

- Started flying after founding his company in 2002.
- Uses best deals on business class, depending on the market situation.
- Collects miles on every system and burns them to take his wife along when possible.
- Buys tickets on the Internet (arranged by the secretary).

The Nifty Corporate Travel Manager

- Fifty-eight year old sourcing veteran in any company on a sharp austerity course.
- Does not fly any more, as sellers have to come and to see her now.
- Has a target to cut corporate spend on travel by 50 percent.
- Downgraded airline, hotel, and rental car standards to coach, Holiday Inn, and subcompact respectively.
- Negotiated corporate net rates for all trunk routes, frequently used hotels, and preferred car rental company.
- Forces internal users to book through company intranet site.
- Reports cost deviations to the Chief Financial Officer.
- Uses online auctions as a negotiating tool.
- Received a $115,000 bonus for not just making, but exceeding her target.

The New Leisure and VFR Travelers

The Florida Golden Age Golfer

- Sixty-two year old "golden handshake" retiree from Boston.
- Bought nice property on golf course in Boca Raton.
- Used to heavily fly business class around the country.
- Now uses jetBlue to see son's family in New York and "burns" his former miles to see daughter's family in San Diego.
- Buys tickets on the Internet.

The Brussels Backpacker

- Twenty-three year old assistant to a Danish politician, assigned to the European Commission.
- Takes one overseas trip every year in summer and spends weekends with chat-pals around Europe (around 5 trips per year).
- Traveled on EuroRail pass during High School.
- Now uses bargain deals (mainly Emirates or Qatar for Asia travel, KLM for North and Middle America and Ryanair out of Charleroi for Europe).
- Uses the Internet to find best deals.

The Stanford Student

- Twenty-four year old studies Industrial Engineering, likes traveling, and has a father who is a well-off lawyer.
- Travels to Asia, South America and every three months to see family in New Jersey.
- No former travel experience.
- Uses dad's miles for long haul travel and Priceline to find deals for domestic travel.
- Uses the Internet for bookings.

The Turkish Taylor from Berlin

- Forty-one year old, runs a successful small business in the western outskirts of Berlin.
- Used to fly "home" twice a year on "ethnic charters" operated by mostly "Fly-By-Night" airlines.
- Now flies whenever he likes to his home town of Istanbul on Germania Express' daily service.
- Buys tickets in nearby Turkish travel agency.

The Shanghai School Teacher

- Forty-seven year old English teacher in a private language school with a husband (who works at hotel reception desk) and one son.
- Family income of $35,000 a year.
- Never left China until 2003.
- Now visits cousins in Vancouver, Canada every year.
- Flies in economy class on Air China.
- Buys tickets in a downtown travel agency after consulting the Internet at school to find most suitable days.

As evident, the lack of homogeneity in the airlines' customer base is significant. In the category of "Business Travelers", we see young professionals from developing countries, typical US "Road Warriors", management staff that had been downgraded to economy class by corporate rules, well paid specialists, and captains of industry. All have different priorities on their agenda. In the leisure-VFR category, we find first time travelers from China, backpackers from Australia, wealthy pensioners from Europe, Polish-American families, and so forth. The list of driving factors could be enlarged by:

- The growing influence of the intranet based corporate travel systems that reduce the airline choices of travelers in order to fulfill turnover commitments in corporate travel deals.

- The fact that many industrialized countries see a growing amount of "social downgrading" within North American and European societies as the number of middle class families decline and lower class incomes stagnate due to global competition for lower and middle qualification jobs. Although the growing wealth of the top class may tend to blur the statistics, the trends are still evident.

To recap, the impact of the aforementioned customer and business trends within the airline industry as well as the rapid growth and embracement of the Internet has changed passenger behavior and decision criteria dramatically. Passengers now feel empowered to select the price-service combination they want. Passengers on business travel, in particular, can now *see* the fare premium they paid for virtually, in some cases, a commodity product. Transparency of fares and services produced by the Internet has enabled passengers to become sophisticated and empowered, taking advantage of loopholes in the complex fare systems. Technology has also led to a dramatic shift in the distribution channel (as discussed in detail in Chapter 6). Passengers can now buy in different ways and in different places reducing airline revenues. In addition, *surfing* on the Internet has provided consumers not only the capability to create their own customized packages encompassing all of their travel needs, but has also created, to some extent, demand for certain destinations.

The pace and impact of technology change seems to have had an impact on the demand for air travel in both directions. While airlines have always benefited from the need for face-to-face meeting—there is some evidence that this need is undergoing a change. The cell phone with video is becoming ubiquitous. Internet data and voice telephony are making, for a few people, the whole concept of "long distance" a distant memory. This development, combined with High Definition Television (HDTV) and high quality sound reproduction could make electronic meetings between people in far-apart cities intimate and accessible.

On the other hand, there are young business people with their "now—no waiting" approach to problem solving. They are just as likely to open up an internet chat room with customers or suppliers, or to use a HDTV hook-up to "see" them face-to-face electronically, or jump on a plane to go and see someone in person to solve a problem or develop an opportunity. They will use technology—electronics or airplane travel—to make things happen faster. Consequently, consumer and business trends will have both a positive and a negative impact on the demand for air travel. The key for airline managements is to focus on aligning customer and business trends with the skills and capabilities of their businesses.

Acknowledging the Customer-Induced Economic Stresses

Macroeconomic Factors

Macroeconomic factors weigh heavily on passengers' experience with airlines. Economic cycles faced by consumers produce overcapacity for airlines during downturns due to the long asset life of aircraft. Overcapacity in downturns becomes an even greater challenge since airline managements tend to over-expand during upswings, as was the case during the mid 1990s. Unfortunately, the recent downturn, beginning in the late 1990s and early 2000, was longer and deeper. During this downturn consumer spending and corporate purchasing power declined much more steeply—placing an enormous squeeze on travel budgets—and the impact is likely to be permanent. Passengers now have sufficient services offered by the unconventional airlines—services that are not only acceptable but, in some cases, even more desirable.

Consider just one example. In the 2005 Airline Customers Satisfaction Index Study (issued on March 14, 2005) by the JD Power Associates, jetBlue ranked number one in a survey based on responses from 2,600 passengers who flew on a major US airline between May and October of 2004.[9] Table 1.1 shows three statistics for unconventional and conventional airlines: the recent JD Power Satisfaction Ranking, the average domestic fare, and the operating profit or loss for the calendar year 2004. The average ranking is based on a straight forward arithmetic average and does not contain any weights representing size or any other airline characteristic. Admittedly, this is too simplistic an analysis. Nevertheless, despite the drawbacks associated with the simplicity of the numbers, one conclusion does stand out. The unconventional airlines have a higher satisfaction score, offer lower fares, and make a larger operating profit.

Both premium fare and lower fare passengers are now focused on value. The marketplace has a broad spectrum of conventional and unconventional airlines, each offering different kinds of value. It is unlikely that significant numbers of business travelers will revert to paying premium fares after the economy recovers from this lingering

Table 1.1   Passenger Satisfaction, Passenger Fare and Airline Profitability

Airline	JD Power Satisfaction Rank	Average Domestic Fare	Operating Profit CY 2004
AirTran	5	$135	$ 32,844,000
jetBlue	1	$152	$ 112,943,000
Southwest	2	$130	$ 554,000,000
Unconventional Airlines	3	$139	$ 699,787,000
Alaska	4	$193	$ (85,400,000)
America West	10	$179	$ (39,704,000)
American	7	$222	$ (761,000,000)
Continental	6	$230	$ (229,000,000)
Delta	3	$184	$(3,308,000,000)
Northwest	11	$204	$ (505,000,000)
United	9	$216	$ (854,000,000)
US Airways	8	$172	$ (611,000,000)
Conventional Airlines	7	$200	$(6,393,104,000)

Source: JD Power Associates (ranking reported in USA Today April 5, 2005, p. 10B), the US Department of Transportation Data Banks (3rd Quarter 2004 for fare data), and the Airline SEC Financial Reports.

recession—implying that the world of business travelers has changed forever. It is also unlikely that lower fare passengers are willing to pay higher fares. Even more significant may be the following question. Given equal fares, would customers choose to take conventional or unconventional airlines? Would even first class and frequent flyer programs bring back these customers?

Decline in Business Travel

Figure 1.1 shows the decline in the number of business travelers in premium cabins. At the beginning of the 1990s, over 60 percent of business travelers in short haul intra-European sectors traveled in premium cabins. At the end of 2004, the number was closer to 20 percent and could easily drop to 10 percent in the near future—due in part to the fact that while traffic remained constant, leisure traffic grew.

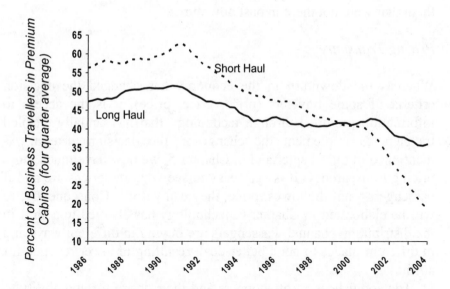

Figure 1.1 Passenger Travel in Premium Cabins
Source: Andrew Sentance (British Airways), Presentation made at The Ohio State University and Continental Airlines 12th International Airline Symposium, January 17-19, 2005, Honolulu, Hawaii, USA.

From passengers' perspective, there are two other factors that have produced an even more serious negative impact on the airline industry. First, during this particular downturn the market experienced consecutive significant shocks such as September 11, 2001, the war in Iraq and SARS. Take just one example of the impact of September 11, 2001. Due to the additional hassles associated with airport security, airlines in the US could be losing up to 25 percent of their short haul business, even though the overall domestic market is back to September 11, 2001 levels. Second, while corporations took actions to reduce their travel budgets as they have done in previous downturns, many corporations remained cost conscious even when the economy started to show signs of improvement. In addition, as some unconventional airlines provide greater legroom, fewer fare restrictions and greater entertainment options, travelers are happier with the lower fare options available to them that were not there in past downturns.

Pricing Transparency

Whereas the downturn in the economy has changed the decision criteria of some travelers (price, price, price), it is the access to information provided through technology that has actually enabled travelers to implement the change in the decision criteria. As mentioned in this chapter and in Chapter 5, we now have much more pricing transparency. It is very easy to see what the prices are and if passengers want the lowest price, they can get it.[10] Consequently, as will be elaborated in Chapter 6, technology has also led to a shift in the distribution channel. Passengers are buying in different ways and in different places to get a better deal, resulting in lower revenue for airlines.

The sophistication of shoppers and their desire for and ability to find lower fares (resulting from the economic pressures and the availability of the Internet) has resulted in an unprecedented and fundamental shift in the structure of fares. In the US, the level of average fares has continued to decline and the total passenger revenue as a fraction of the total GDP took a sharp decline beginning around the year 2000. Figure 1.2 shows the relationship between the revenue earned by the US airline industry (all airlines with annual revenue over US$100 million) and the US GDP. In the 20 year period, between 1980 and the year 2000, airline passenger revenue as a percent of US GDP ranged between 0.8 and 1.0 percent. It has been declining in the past four years. Similar trends are seen in other countries. See, for example, Figure 1.3 that shows a similar relationship between the revenue of British Airways and the UK GDP.[11] The structural change in the dynamics of consumer demand appears to have resulted in an irreversible downward pressure on passenger yields, at least in the US domestic and intra-European markets. Surveys show a significant change in the traffic mix, as for example in Europe, where a much greater percentage of passengers now travel on economy class fares. This change in traffic mix coupled with a reduction in economy fares provides a good explanation of the decline in the industry wide yield.[12]

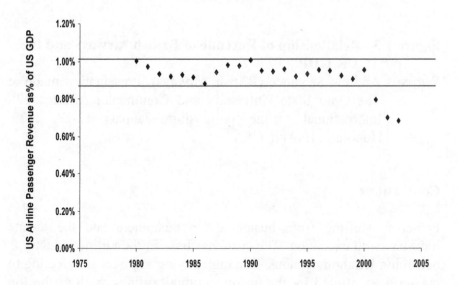

Figure 1.2   Relationship between the US Airline Industry Revenue and US GDP

Source: Drawn on the data extracted from the Website of the Air Transport Association of America.

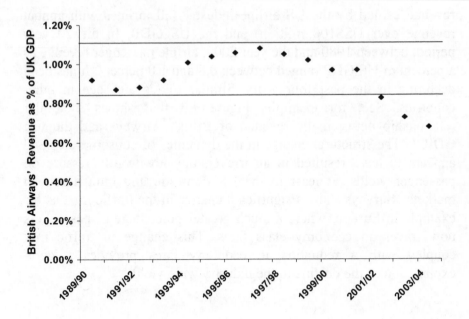

Figure 1.3   Relationship of Revenue of British Airways and the UK GDP

Source: Andrew Sentance (British Airways), Presentation made at The Ohio State University and Continental Airlines 12th International Airline Symposium, January 17-19, 2005, Honolulu, Hawaii, USA.

Conclusions

Power is shifting from businesses to customers and the airline industry is no exception. The customer base in the airline industry is becoming less homogenous. The high paying segment is defecting to the services offered by the unconventional airlines, both at the top end (corporate jets) and at the low end (low fare airlines). Examine, for example, the behavior of our New Hampshire Netjetter and the DaimlerChrysler Detroit Shuttler at one end, and the London City Business Banker and the Silicon Valley Coach Consultant at the other.   All sub-segments now have different priorities on their agenda, resulting in the almost impossible task of gaining customer insights for segmentation (discussed in Chapter 3) and the use of traditional market research techniques (discussed in Chapter 8).

Premium fare and lower fare passengers are now focused on value. However, despite the generation of "price, price and price", a significant portion of airline customers have the desire, interest and capability to trade up to a higher level of service, accompanied by higher fares. However, improvements in service must represent meaningful innovations and provide actual or perceived value. The change in consumer behavior, the downturn in the economy and the expansion of technology has changed the decision criteria of some segments of travelers. Shoppers are now much more sophisticated. Airlines must now learn to make "the right offer, to the right customer, at the right time".

Notes

[1] Ettenberg, Elliott, *The Next Economy: Will You Know Where Your Customers Are?* (New York: McGraw-Hill, 2002), pp. 49, 59.

[2] Stinnett, Bill, *Think Like Your Customers: A Winning Strategy to Maximize Sales by Understanding How and Why Your Customers Buy* (New York: McGraw-Hill, 2005), p. 5.

[3] Hill, Sam, *Sixty Trends in Sixty Minutes* (Hoboken, NJ: John Wiley & Sons, 2002), p. 124.

[4] Silverstein, Michael J. and Neil Fiske, *Trading Up: The New American Luxury* (New York: Portfolio, Penguin Group, 2003), p. 38.

[5] Spector, Robert, *Category Killers: The Retail Revolution and Its Impact on Consumer Culture* (Boston, MA: Harvard University Press, 2005), p. xiii.

[6] Silverstein, Michael J. and Neil Fiske, *Trading Up: The New American Luxury* (New York: Portfolio, Penguin Group, 2003), p. 10.

[7] Kelly, Eamon and Peter Leyden, W*hat's Next: Exploring the New Terrain for Business* (New York: Global Business Network, 2002), p. 93.

[8] Silverstein, Michael J. and Neil Fiske, *Trading Up: The New American Luxury,* (New York: Portfolio, Penguin Group, 2003), p. 11.

[9] Reed, Dan, "Report says quality of air service slipped in 2004", *USA Today,* April 5, 2005, p. 10B.

[10] Karlgaard, Rich, *Life 2.0: How People Across America Are Transforming Their Lives by Finding the Where of Their Happiness* (New York: Crown Business, 2004).

[11] Part of this trend is the result of the downsizing by British Airways.

[12] Mason, Keith J., "Observations of fundamental changes in the demand for aviation services", *Journal of Air Transport Management*, Volume 11 (2005), pp. 19-25.

Chapter 2

Taking a Bird's Eye View of the Landscape

Whereas the previous chapter explained the changing nature of customer behavior, the diversity of the airline customer base, and the impact of customer-induced economic stresses, this chapter is an overview of the changing landscape—how different aviation organizations are meeting the needs of the changing passengers. The first part provides some examples of the successful products and services introduced by emerging competitors—unconventional businesses—to meet the changing needs of the marketplace. The second part provides an overview of the initiatives taken by the conventional airlines and the varying degrees of success they have had in presenting their new value propositions to (a) slow down the diversion of passengers to the new competitors, and (b) to possibly attract back some of the customers who have already abandoned them.

Recognizing the Successes of Different Aviation Competitors

From the passengers' perspective, the competitive landscape has been changing from both the supply side as well as the demand side. Consider the following three points.

- Deregulation in the United States and Europe and liberalization in other parts of the world created an opportunity for new unconventional airlines to enter the marketplace and offer alternative price-service choices. In Europe, market access was less of an issue, but slots were and still are, a major issue in many key airports. In the Asia-Pacific region, despite the temporary lack of landing rights in some countries, passengers are seeing the growth of unconventional airlines to satisfy the needs of the enormous growth in the middle classes, with some people flying for the first time in their lives.

- The liberalization process has enabled some small conventional network airlines, particularly those based in the Middle East, to expand their operations well beyond what would normally be supported by the size of their own traffic bases to offer alternative price-service options.[1]

- The rise in business fares and deterioration in services provided by commercial airlines has led to an expansion of services provided by suppliers of corporate jet services, such as NetJets. Although the role of business jets in Europe is much smaller (compared to the United States by a ratio of almost 10 to 1), it is increasing as European corporations are beginning to view business jets more as productivity tools and less as luxury items.

Unconventional Airlines

The shift from Price to Value   Consider, first, the benefits obtained by passengers from the proliferation of unconventional airlines. These carriers have used their low costs to offer lower fares—a reality the conventional airlines now have to contend with worldwide. What started in the US and spread to Europe, is now gaining power in Asia and Latin America. Unconventional airlines are also growing very quickly. It was not that long ago that conventional airlines knew about them and did not worry. The unconventional airlines were small enough that the conventional airlines could afford to ignore them and, in turn, the needs of some passengers. This is not true anymore. In the US, the major airlines underestimated the new entrants because, until recently, start-up airlines since deregulation have been, for the most part, purely price driven. jetBlue changed that model by not simply leasing a few old airplanes and charging $59 to fly from the US Northeast to Florida. Consumers have embraced jetBlue's product not so much because it is cheap but rather because it is simply better. Conventional airlines misunderstood and thought they could do what they always did in response—lower fares and dump capacity. They missed the fact that consumers are getting a better product, as well as a lower fare. Consequently, the response of the conventional airlines has been largely ineffective to compete with the value propositions of airlines such as jetBlue, AirTran and Frontier. In some ways, the conventional airlines are still fighting the last war. They have tried to fight on price whereas the new airlines are competing on value.

Based on their value proposition, the new airlines have grown very rapidly. Consider the 20 years it took Southwest to become a major carrier (revenue exceeding a billion dollars). Compare that with how long it took jetBlue—less than four years. Germanwings, the airline created in 2002 by Eurowings, is expanding its fleet from 14 airplanes at the beginning of 2005 to 20 airplanes by the summer of 2005.[2] In India, Jet Airways, Air Sahara, Air Deccan and Kingfisher Airlines could each easily have between 40 and 80 aircraft by 2010. Some of these unconventional airlines are also using their low costs to offer some upscale services/features (cheap frills) to meet the needs of yet another segment of the market.

As an example of the consumer benefits received from the penetration power of an unconventional airline, consider Southwest's services to and from Baltimore, Maryland. In 1991, US Airways (a high fare airline) had a 46 percent share of the O&D traffic to and from Baltimore. Southwest entered the market in 1993. Ten years later, Southwest had captured 44 percent of the share while US Airways' share dropped to a mere 7 percent. It is interesting to note that US Airways introduced its low fare MetroJet service to mirror Southwest's operations but it still failed, partly due to the reason mentioned above: MetroJet simply offered a lower price, not better value. The new subsidiaries being formed in Asia—for example in Singapore and Australia—are likely to succeed because they are not only going to have lower costs but they are also going to offer a better value proposition.

Low Fare Competition Exploding Worldwide   One can also examine the impact of low fare competition in specific markets. Figure 2.1 shows the impact of low fares between the broader Washington (Baltimore, Reagan, and Dulles Airports) and the broader Chicago market (Midway and O'Hare Airports). As the fare came down, traffic increased. However, even though Southwest served only the Baltimore-Midway market, its low fare service had enormous benefits for consumers residing near the sister markets. For example, in 1991, the fare in the Baltimore-Midway market was $186. After Southwest's entry, it dropped to $50 in 1994. However, for the same period, the fare also dropped in the sister market, Baltimore-O'Hare, from $175 to $67.

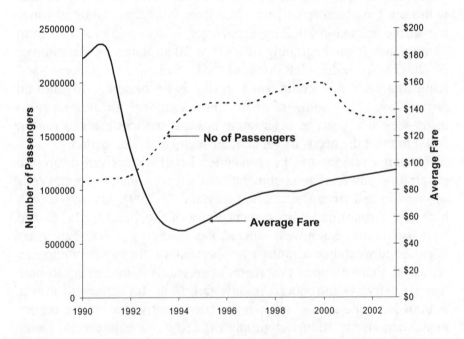

Figure 2.1   Passenger Traffic and Fare Trends in the Greater Washington-Chicago Market

Source: US Department of Transportation Data Banks.

Figure 2.2 shows the benefit of jetBlue's service in the New York, JFK-Los Angeles, Long Beach market (JFK-LAX and JFK-LGB, respectively). First, jetBlue's entry stimulated the market demand in the JFK-LGB market from virtually zero in the third quarter of 2000 to almost 220, 000 in the third quarter 2004. Second, there was not only a reduction in passenger traffic in the sister market, JFK-LAX, of about 3 percent, but also a reduction in fare of 33 percent during the same period. Moreover, the percentage of passengers who paid over $1,000 in the JFK-LAX market fell from 10 percent to 3 percent in the four year period. Consequently, before jetBlue's entry into JFK-LGB, 10 percent of the passengers paid fares that accounted for 41 percent of the revenue. After jetBlue's entry, 3 percent of the passengers who paid the high fare accounted for only 21 percent of the revenue. To summarize, jetBlue's entry in one market led to lower fares and a reduction in traffic in a sister market. In Europe, while there is no comparable data on fares at the market level, similar traffic effects have been reported by Civil Aviation Authorities.

Key Success Factors   The consumer benefit of unconventional airline entry is very similar in other parts of the world. Consider the case of the UK. Figure 2.3 shows the growth of the traffic carried by two unconventional airlines in and out of the UK compared to the traffic carried by British Airways.

From a consumer's perspective, the key success factor of unconventional airlines is their value proposition—the delivery of consistently reliable service at everyday low prices. Contrast this with the conventional airlines who developed two basic segments—less price sensitive and more price sensitive—of the marketplace and practiced significant price discrimination (as explained in Chapter 5). The restrictive fare fences—advance purchase, Saturday night stay, non-refundable fares, round-trip travel—forced business travelers to pay excessive premiums over the fares paid by less constrained travelers. The insupportable price discrimination and the inability to achieve sustainable low operating costs provided an opportunity for unconventional airlines to create an alternative value proposition for both kinds of passengers who paid premium fares for virtually commodity products.[3]

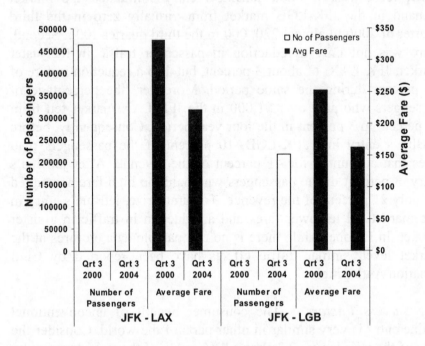

Figure 2.2   Impact of a Low Fare Airline Entry on Traffic and Fares

Source: US Department of Transportation Data Banks.

The unconventional airlines are offering products, for the first time in the new entrants' history, that actually appeal to business travelers. In the US consider, for example, that AirTran allows for $25 upgrades to business class or that jetBlue's 34 inch seat pitch allows business travelers to actually open their laptops, unlike conventional airlines' seats with the typical 31 inch pitch. Based in Singapore, Valuair has positioned itself as a mid-frills carrier, offering value for money. It charges a little more than the ultra low fare airlines but provides comfortable seats, hot meals, baggage allowance, assigned seats, interlining capability and access through its own website or through traditional travel agents. Positioning itself as a mid-frills airline, it compares itself to other industries that offer mid-range products: Toyota in the automobile industry (compared to Mercedes Benz vs. Lada); Swatch in the watch industry (compared to Rolex vs. Casio; and Adidas and Reebok in tennis shoes (compared to Nike vs. Bata).[4]

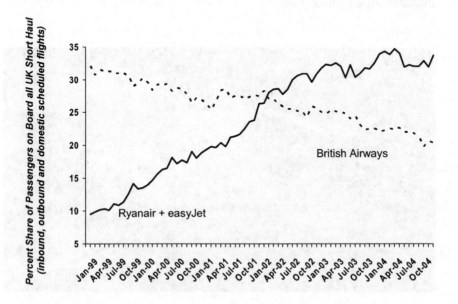

Figure 2.3   Growth of Ryanair+easyJet and British Airways in and out of the UK

Source: Andrew Sentance (British Airways), Presentation made at The Ohio State University and Continental Airlines 12th International Airline Symposium, January 17-19, 2005, Honolulu, Hawaii, USA.

New Conventional Airlines

Besides the unconventional airlines, long haul intercontinental consumers now have access to new products offered by the new conventional airlines (network competitors)—for example, those based in the Middle East. Consider the global route network of

Emirates. See Figure 2.4. This is an enormous network given the size of the home market. As will be discussed in the next chapter, Emirates is already providing alternative services in a huge number of markets and will expand its service globally, given its relatively low costs, excellent geographic location, good brand and relatively unconstrained infrastructure.

Figure 2.4 Network of Emirates Airlines (2004)
Source: Emirates' Website.

Consider the new nonstop flight of Emirates between New York and Dubai. Table 2.1 shows that, according to the airline schedules, passengers from New York can make connections with flights from Dubai to 37 other destinations in the Gulf, in Africa, in Asia and in Australasia.

Although the largest airline based in the Middle East, Emirates is by no means the only up-coming competitor of global airlines. Consider, the networks of Qatar and Etihad, two other relatively new airlines based in countries with tiny home markets. Take Qatar Airways' nonstop flight between London and Doha. Table 2.2 shows that once this flight arrives in Doha, passengers from London can connect to 40 other destinations in the Gulf, Africa and Asia.

Table 2.1 Possible Connections in Dubai with Emirates' New York-Dubai Nonstop Flight—March 2005

New York—Dubai—with connections to

Amman, Jordan	Kuwait, Kuwait
Bahrain, Bahrain	Larnaca, Cyprus
Beirut, Lebanon	Lahore, Pakistan
Bangkok, Thailand	Lagos, Nigeria
Mumbai, India	Chennai, India
Cairo, Egypt	Muscat, Oman
Colombo, Sri Lanka	Malta, Malta
Cochin, India	Male, Maldives
Dhaka, Bangladesh	Manila, Philippines
Delhi, India	Mauritius, Mauritius
Damman, Saudi Arabia	Nairobi, Kenya
Doha, Qatar	Perth, Australia
Hong Kong, Hong Kong	Peshawar, Pakistan
Hyderabad, India	Shanghai, China
Islamabad, Pakistan	Sana, Yemen
Johannesburg, South Africa	Mahe Island, Seychelles
Karachi, Pakistan	Singapore, Singapore
Osaka, Japan	Tehran, Iran
Kuala Lumpur, Malaysia	

Source: March 2005 World Airline Schedules.

Table 2.2   Possible Connections in Doha with Qatar's London-Doha Nonstop Flight—March 2005

London: Heathrow—Doha, Qatar—with connections to

Aden, Yemen	Osaka, Japan
Amman, Jordan	Khartoum, Sudan
Abu Dhabi, UAE	Katmandu, Nepal
Bahrain, Bahrain	Kuala Lumpur, Malaysia
Beirut, Lebanon	Kuwait, Kuwait
Bangkok, Thailand	Lahore, Pakistan
Mumbai, India	Luxor, Egypt
Cairo, Egypt	Muscat, Oman
Jakarta, Indonesia	Male, Maldives
Colombo, Sri Lanka	Manila, Philippines
Cochin, India	Beijing, China
Dhaka, Bangladesh	Peshawar, Pakistan
Damascus, Syria	Shanghai, China
Damman, Saudi Arabia	Yangon, Myanmar
Dubai, UAE	Riyadh, Saudi Arabia
Hyderabad, India	Sana, Yemen
Islamabad, Pakistan	Mahe Island, Seychelles
Jeddah, Saudi Arabia	Singapore, Singapore
Johannesburg, South Africa	Tehran, Iran
Karachi, Pakistan	Trivandrum, India

Source: March 2005 World Airline Schedules.

The fleets ordered by these new carriers based in the Middle East could create overcapacity, leading to lower fares—clearly a benefit to passengers, at least in the short term. These new carriers can support the lower fares based partly on their lower costs—labor, airport charges and possibly fuel, not to mention that their plans are part of their countries' integrated economic and political development. The real benefit will be for passengers who have to make a stop anyway, for example, between London and Sydney. Another factor that could lead to excessive price competition (again, in the interest of passengers) is the close proximity of the hubs of the Middle East based airlines to one another. Again, the real beneficiaries of these airlines will be passengers, for example, the European passengers traveling to Asia and the US passengers traveling to the Middle East.

Corporate Jet Services

Consumers are also benefiting from the products of organizations providing fractional ownerships in jets. NetJets is the dominant fractional jet ownership company with a fleet of 550 aircraft (as of March 2005), raging from the light cabin Citation Bravos to the large cabin Airbus and Boeing jets. It is interesting to note that in terms of fleet size only, NetJets operates a fleet larger than all the US major passenger airlines, except American. The services provided are ideal for the well-heeled passengers who not only do not want the hassle of flying on commercial aircraft but also prefer the security and privacy associated with corporate jets.

Since fractional jet ownership is still expensive, in June 2001, Marquis Jet Partners joined forces with NetJets and introduced 25-hour cards that allow users to purchase 25 hours of flight time on a given type of aircraft.[5] Additional hours can be purchased in increments of five hours. Prices for the 25-hour card can range from €115,000 for the Citation Bravo to €340,000 for the Gulfstream V.[6] The advantage of using prepaid cards is that the user does not pay for such costs as aircraft positioning and crew dead-heading. Aircraft are available on a 24/7 basis with only 10 hours of advanced notice required. The popularity of the card is evident from the fact that it was only introduced in 2001 and already there are almost 1,400 Marquis Jet card owners.

A second example is Bombardier's Flexjet, that started in May 2004. It is a fixed price trans-Atlantic service business jet using the company's Global Express airplanes. The cost is reported to be about €150,000. A full ten-seat aircraft results in a round trip trans-Atlantic fare of £10,000. The demand for such services comes from a variety of sources such as the retirement of Concorde and the ability of the corporate aircraft to access numerous small convenient airports such as New Jersey's Teterboro Airport.[7]

A third example changing the competitive landscape is the Switzerland based PrivatAir that is an operator flying on behalf of network airlines. This company started operating trans-Atlantic flights for Lufthansa and Swiss International Airlines in 45-55 seat single aisle jets under a wet lease contract. The company also operates a scheduled shuttle for Airbus' own operations (employees, suppliers and customers), connecting the aircraft manufacturer's widespread facilities, as well as conventional charter business jets..

The fourth example of the expanding use of corporate and regional jets is corporate shuttles. For reasons discussed below, some of these corporations are turning to the use of corporate shuttles operated by external organizations, specialized companies or regional airlines. The use of corporate shuttles is saving money, for example, by staff avoiding overnight stays due to poor commercial services in thinner markets. It is increasing productivity by enabling staff to be able to work on board. It is improving the quality of life due to a significant reduction in the hassle factor, higher levels of security and by enabling passengers to be home more nights. Corporate shuttle activity is forecast to increase in light of the increasing needs to transport large or predictable numbers of staff on a regular basis. One example of a high visibility corporate shuttle is Daimler-Chrysler's weekday operations of a 319 between Stuttgart, Germany and Pontiac, Michigan, USA. Shuttles have proven to be an extremely successful value proposition for the executives and staff of the organizations that operate them. These are examples of premium paying passengers who are not coming back.

Recognizing the Initiatives of Conventional Airlines

Although it was the business model of the conventional airlines that produced significant levels of dissatisfaction for consumers, the conventional airlines have taken limited steps that have helped a little, though from the passengers' perspective, they have a long way to go. Historically, conventional airlines developed a business model where a passenger could travel rather seamlessly between virtually any two points in the world. This business model incorporated an enormous complexity of internal process, infrastructure, industry standards and relationships among airlines as well as with numerous external aviation organizations and stakeholders. Although most conventional airlines took far too long to acknowledge that the past business model was no longer working, they have now begun the process of changing the business model starting with massive cost reductions, changes in various components of marketing and changes in organizational structure and culture. The initiatives taken by some leading conventional airlines embraced two basic criteria—simplification and standardization—a reduction in the number of fare types, the use of more direct distribution, reductions in the number and complexity of fleet types and simplified service options, especially on short haul services. They have also automated previously staffed functions, and are unbundling the product-price offer, charging for items previously included. Unfortunately for conventional airlines, unconventional airlines continue to play to their strengths—stay focused on core competencies, provide value for money and manage customer expectations—to keep diverting passengers to their services. In the following paragraphs are examples of the initiatives taken by conventional airlines to position their services to meet the changing needs of the marketplace.

Organizational Changes

Consolidation is seen as one solution to the twin structural problem of the global airline industry—overcapacity and increased competition from unconventional airlines. In Europe, for example, conventional airlines with small home markets and high operating costs cannot compete head to head with the three major European carriers. As a result, the consolidation process finally began when in 2004 the French and the Dutch governments approved the linkage between Air France and KLM, creating the largest airline in the world with annual revenue of almost US$25 billion. By leveraging each airline's strengths (for example, coordinating traffic through their respective hubs and eliminating duplications in network), the Franco-Dutch merged airline is beginning to show signs of reductions in costs and an improvement in profitability. It is interesting to note that for the Air France-KLM group a continuing challenge is the lack of profitability of domestic routes. The reason for that is not so much competition from unconventional airlines but more from the aggressive pricing strategies of the French Railway System (SNCF). For example, train fares between Paris and Marseilles are reportedly as low as $38, an amount less than just the airport and security taxes paid by air travelers on this route.[8]

In March 2005, the Boards of both Lufthansa and Swiss International approved the acquisition of Swiss International by Lufthansa. Just as the Air France-KLM merger enabled the combined airline to rationalize its combined network (the hub operations at Paris' Charles de Gaulle and Amsterdam's Schiphol Airports), the Lufthansa and Swiss combination will enable Lufthansa to have greater access to the market of Switzerland, some rationalization in cross-border network (for example, flights between Switzerland and Germany as well as improved connectivity across their three hubs—Frankfurt, Munich, and Zurich), corporate sales and frequent flyer programs. Whereas, consolidation within the airline industry in the US has had a poor track record, mergers in Europe promise to be more successful—using as a model the concept of one control group but two remaining separate airlines—by specifically avoiding labor integration, an area that proved to be a real problem in the US.[9]

Cost Reductions

Almost 80 percent of the US domestic markets have competitive services offered by unconventional airlines with lower costs. For the year June 30, 2001 (before all the major problems), if the nine major US airlines had the costs per available seat mile (CASM) of Southwest Airlines, their costs would have been US$18.7 billion lower for their domestic operations.[10] Consequently, the major focus of the conventional airlines has been related to reducing their costs to survive, more than producing customer driven systems.

The cost reduction initiatives of conventional airlines have been applied across the board, exemplified by:

- Renegotiating labor rates and contract provisions.

- Introducing low-cost subsidiaries.

- Reducing the number of fleet types and overhauling the fleet scheduling criteria.

- Encouraging direct distribution channels, partly to reduce costs and partly to "get closer to the customer".

- Closing unprofitable parts of the network, including, in some cases, hubs.

- Introducing more self-service options, partly to reduce costs and partly to provide more options for passengers.

- Changing the decision criterion for operations (for example, crew and aircraft routings and irregular operations) from higher revenue/higher costs to lower costs/higher profits.

The approach to labor cost reduction has varied within the industry. In the US, management focused on lower wages. In Europe, it appears that Lufthansa followed a strategy of "more work for the same pay". British Airways increased the use of franchise operations, not just on regional routes but also on some mainline routes—for example, pulling out full size jets from Manchester and having GB Airways operate with the 320s from Manchester in BA colors. Although the cost reductions achieved to date have not made the conventional airlines profitable, they have created, at least in the near term, some "staying power". The ability to offer and protect important services with marginal economics has enabled some carriers to stay, and compete, in key markets rather than exit the market. However, the initiatives of many conventional airlines, thus far, represent mostly panic rather than a major mindset change, some exceptions being Aer Lingus, Air Canada, Air New Zealand and British Airways who have all moved forward with significant, even radical, overhauls of their business designs.

Marketing Initiatives

To be fair, having recognized inconsistency and irrationality of fare structures as perceived by consumers, conventional airlines in North America and Europe have begun to simplify their fare structure by eliminating requirements such as Saturday night stay, introducing one way fares and placing caps on top end fares. Take the case of the changes introduced by Air Canada as an example of customer focused strategies. Table 2.3 shows that Air Canada reduced its fare options to six categories, with different conditions. Passengers could clearly see the price-service options on the airline's website with a reasonable degree of transparency.

Since the simplification of its price-service options, Air Canada realized that passengers wanted it to go even further with changes. Air Canada again revised its price-service options in the Spring of 2005, as shown in Table 2.4. It eliminated one fare option and restrictions relating to the length of stay.

The aforementioned strategies appear to have slowed the gain in market share by the unconventional airlines. A la carte pricing—a consumer desired feature—is also becoming more common. Some airlines have gone to ticketing fees if a passenger chooses to buy the ticket in the reservations office or at the ticket counter. Some are charging for meals. One is reportedly charging a fee for the use of skycaps at selected airports. Ryanair has used this strategy to sell everything. The fare for the basic flight product is low, but every other incremental product or service element must be paid for. The important sources of revenue appear to be excess baggage and credit card fees.

Although conventional airlines are aggressively pursuing the direct distribution channel, they are continuing to sell in almost all places and in every way—every channel. There are, however, differences in how they are relating to the customer in various channels with various costs of service. As to the websites, while

Table 2.3   Air Canada's Old Price-Service Options

	Tango	Fun	Latitude	Freedom	Executive Class	Econo
Changes:	Unlimited - $25	Unlimited - $25	Unlimited – Free	Unlimited – Free	Unlimited – Free	Unlimited $75
Refundable:	Non-Refundable	Non-Refundable	√	√	√	Non-Refundabl
Advance Purchase:	May apply	0 – 14 Days	None	None	None	3-7 Days
Minimum Stay:	None	None	None	None	None	Saturday Ni
Same Day Standby	Not Permitted	Not Permitted	√	√	√	Not Permitt
Aeroplane Status Miles:	50% non-status	50%	100%	125%	125%	50%
Web Exclusive:	√	√	-	-	-	-
Priority Check-in:	-	-	-	√	√	-
Priority Boarding:	-	-	-	√	√	-
Priority Baggage Handling:	-	-	-	√	√	-
Access to Maple Leaf Lounges:	-	-	-	√	√	-

Source: Air Canada Website.

unconventional airlines have websites that are much simpler than those of the conventional airlines, while the latter appear to have gone for full functionality solutions that had made the websites somewhat cluttered and a little harder to navigate. Consumers have rewarded airlines that offer simple fare structures and easy online booking tools by buying tickets online in huge numbers. It is also worth noting that one global airline has produced such a user friendly website and gained the trust of consumers to the degree that it has been able to persuade consumers to "buy up", resulting in a 2 percent increase in its yield.

Table 2.4   Air Canada's New Price-Service Options

	Tango	Tango Plus	Latitude	Latitude Plus	Executive Class
Changes:	$30 - 150[4]	$30 – 50[4]	Unlimited – Free	Unlimited – Free	Unlimited – Free
Refundable:	Non-Refundable	Non-Refundable	√	√	√
Advance Seat Selection:	$15	0 – 14 Days	None	None	None
Separate Claim:	-	-	-	√	None
Upgrade Eligibility:	-	√[3]	√[3]	√[3]	√
Aeroplane Status Miles:	50% non-status	50%	100%	125%	125 - 150%
Online Booking:	√[5]	√[5]	√[5]	√[5]	√[5]
Priority Check-in:	-	-	-	√[2]	√
Priority Boarding:	-	-	-	√[2]	√
Priority Baggage Handling:	-	-	-	√	√
Access to Maple Leaf Lounges:	-	-	-	√[2]	√

1. Varies by booking class
2. Canada only
3. Space available with certificate
4. Time dependent
5. One mile/$1 Spent when booking online

Source: Air Canada's Website.

The conventional airlines, particularly those with global brands, have begun to deploy increasing degrees of personalization for their high value customers. These are particular items to provide some differentiation for an airline's best customers, strengthen loyalty and produce benefits that are not replicable by the low-cost competition. Following are some examples.

- Special reservations telephone numbers which not only answer quickly, but are answered by knowledgeable staff who know the top customers, are able to react quickly and are empowered to resolve the customer's concerns.

- Separate and expedited processing at airports including terminals, separate check-in and security lines and a priority boarding sequence.

- Preferential seating that reserves prime seats for high value passengers and ensures their needs are met, even if they book at the last minute.

Long Term Profit Orientation

Although all of the aforementioned cost reduction and marketing related initiatives have helped, according to some passengers they are still variations on existing themes and few conventional airlines have explored radically different business designs to position themselves in the dramatically-changed, customer-driven and hyper-competitive marketplace (see the discussion in the next chapter). In other words, the cost reduction strategies, coupled with changes in the marketing strategies, have enabled conventional airlines to survive in the short term but they are still not providing products and services desired by passengers—for example, more reasonable fares in business class cabins in intercontinental markets, more nonstop flights and reasonable change fees. Even the recent fare alignment has not eliminated the consumer perception that conventional airlines' pricing structure, with its change fees varying by market and continued restrictions, is not as fair as the pricing structure offered by unconventional airlines.

For conventional airlines, the short term objective has been to reduce costs as much as possible and as quickly as possible. With respect to the long term, however, the object is, of course, not cost minimization or revenue maximization, but rather, profit maximization. The fulfillment of this objective requires greater customer orientation. There is no single answer for the customer orientation strategies—no one way to be successful. Each airline must find the optimal cost-revenue structure for its own business model for its targeted customers, not only to achieve low costs but also to generate value for its market segment. It is doubtful that most conventional airlines can get their costs down to the level of unconventional airlines. They should not even try for parity. Rather, their objective instead should be to restore a CASM-RASM equilibrium within an acceptable percentage range versus the unconventional airlines and the number can vary among the business designs of different airlines, being as little as 10 percent for some and as much as 30 percent for others, depending on the product, distribution, brand and other variables.

The achievement of this goal has been difficult for many conventional airlines due to their inability to bring about a change in culture. Most conventional airlines took far too long to accept that post September 11, 2001 recovery was not just round the corner and simply waiting out the storm was not a reasonable strategy. They took too long to acknowledge a structural change in the dynamics of consumer demand. A few conventional airlines have still not learned to manage prudently through recessions, evidenced by the fact that they have continued to work with old strategies that focused on preserving market share and market presence (dumping capacity and matching fares), relying on simple mass marketing initiatives and working with cross-functionally uncoordinated networks.

Conclusions

The aviation marketplace has experienced a fundamental change, not only as a result of continuing change in consumer behavior discussed in the previous chapter, but also as a result of the unusual economic stresses as well as the dramatic increase in the breadth and depth of competition. Although the initiatives taken by the conventional airlines—cost reductions and changes in marketing—have helped airlines to survive in the short term, they have not helped them to take on the degree of customer orientation needed to survive in the long run. For that they need to explore radically different business designs, based not simply on matching fares but on establishing customer oriented value propositions.

Notes

1   A somewhat similar trend appeared when KLM and Singapore expanded their operations many years.

2   Done, Kevin, "Airlines set to test rivals in Europe", *Financial Times*, March 15, 2005, p. 22.

3   A number of unconventional airlines also price discriminate, albeit from a lower base. For example, the nearer the departure date a passenger books, the higher the fare the passenger is likely to pay.

4   Based on a presentation made at the *2005 Unisys Travel and Transportation Conference*, "Transportation's New Paradigm: Simplifying the Business", sponsored by Cathay Pacific and Unisys, April 12, 2005, Hong Kong.

5   Shinzawa, Fluto, "Fractional Ownership", *Robb Report: For the Luxury Lifestyle*, January 2004, p. 86.

6   "NetJets: dominating the fractional ownership market", *Aviation Strategy*, July/August 2004, pp. 3-5.

7   "NetJets: dominating the fractional ownership market", *Aviation Strategy*, July/August 2004, pp. 3-5.

8   Sparaco, Pierre, "Big Merger Paying Off", *Aviation Week & Space Technology*, January 10, 2005, pp. 52-53.

9   In My 2005, America West and US Airways announced their plans to merge. America West is a smaller, lower cost airline whereas US Airways is a larger, higher cost airline. The stated objective is to create a full service nationwide airline with the pricing structure of a low fare airline. See Carey, Susan and Melanie Trottman, "America West, US Air Make a Deal", *Wall Street Journal*, May 20, 2005, p. A3.

10 *Unisys R2A Scorecard*, Volume 1, Issue 1, October 2002, p. 15.

Chapter 3

Designing Viable Business Models

Passengers are fed up with conventional airlines which fail to deliver value. By trying to be all things to all passengers, many conventional airlines are satisfying only a few passengers. Price sensitive passengers feel that they are paying for services they do not really value. Passengers paying premium fares feel that they are not receiving value commensurate with the high fares they pay. Since many business passengers do not pay for their travel themselves, what really counts is a schedule (high frequency, nonstop services) that saves time, as long as the travel guidelines of their companies are respected. Unconventional airlines, on the other hand, are succeeding because they are focused on providing, not just low fares, but also consistent value for targeted customer segments. Successful unconventional airlines have a clearly thought out and focused business design and have had the discipline to reject non-valued products or services. This chapter discusses the need for some dramatic changes, mostly for conventional airlines, if they are to regain the passengers they have lost and to retain the passengers they still have.

Fragmenting and Segmenting the Customer-Driven Marketplace

Taking a Fresh Look

The key to delivering value is a successful business design which in turn is based on strategic segmentation, a basic marketing concept that airlines have understood for years. For years, conventional airlines' traditional marketing programs have attempted to offer different products to different segments. For example, premium passengers were pampered in first class cabins, rewarded with benefits from their frequent flyer programs (FFPs), and secluded from the masses in airport lounges. However, today's premium travelers in short and medium haul markets feel they are not getting value for money and some product features such as FFPs appear to have lost luster (as ticket prices are coming down, the perceived value of getting a free ticket suffers). Moreover, cutbacks in onboard amenities to reduce costs have further alienated premium passengers.

Before beginning a discussion on segmentation, targeting and positioning, some background on the current situation will be helpful. Price conscious passengers also have new expectations regarding value and are seeking out alternatives to the conventional airlines, but, unlike their predecessors, the latest generation of unconventional airlines is delivering value. Earlier generations of unconventional airlines offered low prices, but a very inconsistent service. Those early unconventional airlines struggled to develop a loyal customer base in the face of stiff competition from the conventional airlines. No longer can a traditional airline fight back low fare competition by reducing prices and increasing capacity until the new airline disappears. Today's unconventional airlines are much different and better competitors than the older generation of unconventional airlines.

The newer generation of successful unconventional airlines provides consistent value and a different travel experience. As a result, unconventional airlines in North America and Europe have been able to win a significant share from the conventional airlines. In the US, about 30 percent of the capacity in domestic markets is now offered by unconventional airlines. In Europe, the number varies by country. The capacity share of the unconventional airlines to and from the UK is about 40 percent (or about 28 percent if charter flights are included) and to and from Germany about 20 percent (including charter flights). It is, therefore, important to keep in mind that the traffic carried by unconventional airlines comes partly from the diversion from conventional airlines and partly from the stimulated traffic.

While the need for conventional airlines to segment and target the marketplace is not new, what is new is the urgency with which conventional airlines must undertake rigid analyses of their markets, customers and core competencies. More importantly, today's passengers are increasingly aware of the many alternatives to conventional airline products, services and prices, and the Internet has empowered today's passengers to seek out the best value for each particular trip. As a result, conventional airlines are struggling. The unconventional airlines cannot become complacent. In Europe, for example, not only the conventional airlines but also the charter airlines are fighting back to protect their market share. Consequently, the unconventional airlines are under pressure not only to reduce their costs even further but also to explore different ways to generate additional revenue—more passengers and additional revenue from existing passengers.

As discussed in the previous chapter, in their attempts to fight back, the conventional airlines have undertaken exhaustive analyses, and proposed modest changes in their business designs. For example, Delta closed its Dallas/Fort Worth hub and redeployed aircraft to its huge Atlanta hub, which in turn was redesigned to become a rolling hub with a constant flow of arrivals and departures throughout the day to smooth out the peaks and valleys of activity. However, simply closing a hub or grounding one or two fleet types is not nearly enough to save conventional airlines in today's changing marketplace. Similarly, since customers prefer nonstop flights (as demonstrated by unconventional airlines), improving connecting times or some costs may not be enough. Eventually, the successful conventional airlines in today's changing marketplace will completely rethink the results of their analyses and successfully implement radically different strategies.

Business Design Considerations

What is required in today's customer-driven marketplace is a business design that is more narrowly designed to provide value for specific target segments. Consequently, some conventional airlines must divest substantial portions of their network and corporate infrastructure and focus on just one or a few target segments. Conventional airlines no longer have the luxury of trying to serve all possible customer segments because the unconventional airlines are prospering in market niches where unfocused conventional airlines are not providing sufficient customer value. Clearly to follow this model implies changes to the organization that are drastic and dramatic. There is no denying the temptation to identify the synergies in multiple segments and attempt to use the same production system. Undoubtedly, for example, it would be difficult to make a business-only airline work in many markets because business traffic cannot be stimulated by any significant amount and there are many directional unbalances. Sticking to this one segment alone would generate very low load factors and the temptation might be to fill up the empty seats with price-sensitive traffic.

The key to long term survival for most conventional airlines is to simultaneously manage one or more independent airline operations serving unique niches matched to the airlines' competitive strengths. Although prior attempts by conventional airlines to manage separate airline operations have had poor results, the basic business model of separate operating subsidiaries targeting separate customer segments is sound and is applicable to the airline industry. Successful airlines do learn from the past. Just as it took years for the refinement of a successful model for an unconventional airline, successful conventional airlines will learn from their own mistakes, and from other industries, how to develop and implement independent products and services for targeted segments.

Some of today's leading conventional airlines are completely rethinking their business design, which entails divesting assets and services that do not add value to the target segment(s) and focusing all remaining resources on the optimal target segment(s). Only a few large international conventional airlines (such as Lufthansa) may be able to operate several subsidiaries targeting specific target segments. Models from other industries include the Marriott Hotel chain (Ritz Carleton, Renaissance, Courtyard, Residence Inn and so forth) and the Swatch Group (from the basic range Swatch, to the mid range Tissot, to the high range Longines, to the prestige Omega). Each company has separate subsidiaries and brands providing products and services to different target segments. Similarly, the optimal business design for an airline depends on its competitive strengths and customer segments it can profitably serve.

Unlike prior attempts at operating airlines-within-airlines, the new business designs for conventional airlines are radically different and laser-focused on specific target segments. The separate subsidiaries are designed, managed and operated independently of each other. Examples include the low-cost subsidiaries of Air New Zealand (Domestic Express) and Qantas (JetStar). By maintaining near complete independence among the separate operating subsidiaries, each remains focused solely on its target segment and avoids the temptation to offer non-valued products and services.

The steps in a radical makeover of a conventional airline's business design are:

- Identify clusters of markets/customer segments that can be served profitably.

- Develop an optimal business design to serve the targeted markets/customer segments.

- Abandon all other markets/customer segments that do not fit one's business designs, or link with those able to do so more efficiently—such as offering rail connections to long haul European flights instead of high cost flights operated by conventional airlines in short haul markets..

Reevaluating the Strategy

Obviously, this process requires a complete re-thinking of existing markets, processes, network, strategies, and tactics. What drives such massive reassessment of business strategies is the permanent and profound shift in the relationship between airlines and customers.

Successful airlines identify and adhere to such optimal business designs, exemplified by the experience of Southwest in the US, Aer Lingus in Ireland, and Virgin Atlantic in the UK. The segmentation element of an optimal business design in a competitive, customer-driven marketplace results from:

- The rigorous analyses of market conditions.

- The complete understanding of customers' expectations and perceptions of value.

- The honest assessment of an airline's own core competencies and weaknesses.

The conceptual framework shown in Figure 3.1 provides a brief overview of an example of the type of analysis that could be undertaken as a first step of the optimal business design. The conceptual framework presented here does not attempt to be all inclusive, but rather sets out the bare essentials. Although the framework may appear to be simplistic, the process of thoroughly evaluating the marketplace, customers and competitive strengths may take months and require enormous resources. However, only by going through this process can an airline—conventional or unconventional—hope to identify an optimal business design. Take the case of unconventional airlines. To begin with, there are some markets even they cannot serve profitably even after taking stimulation into consideration. Next, as the markets they penetrate and stimulate mature they must reevaluate their marketing strategies.[1]

For years, planners and analysts at airlines of all types and sizes have used the basic concepts in this framework to identify opportunities, analyze performance and assess developments, albeit with a much more limited strategic focus than what is required today. The core tenant of the model—a thorough understanding of the (a) marketplace, (b) customer segments and (c) core competencies—is as relevant now as it has ever been. Although understanding competencies is important to understand the starting point, it is important to project those competencies into the future. That is, airlines must develop their competencies in line with what it takes to succeed in a specific segment, again with an honest assessment of the

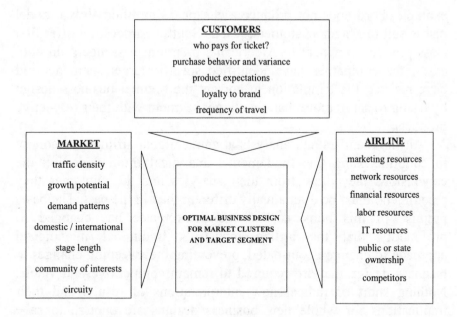

Figure 3.1 Conceptual Framework for Segmentation

difficulty and likelihood involved. The framework is re-introduced here as a reminder of the urgency with which conventional airlines must re-examine their core business design. More importantly, a review of the framework leads into a discussion of how the results of the analyses must now be interpreted differently and whole new business designs must evolve for conventional airlines who hope to prosper in the customer-driven marketplace.

Taking a Different Approach

Indeed, the success of conventional airlines will be determined by their ability to take the results of this analysis and (a) target specific customer segments, and (b) develop differentiated business designs that profitably serve the target segments. In addition, successful conventional airlines will possess the discipline to not stray from the optimal business design in pursuit of other customer segments. For example, Ford does not produce a cheaper, simplified Volvo model just to sell to Mazda customers, just as Southwest does not offer first class product to appeal to American's premium passengers. In both cases, the companies have identified specific target segments and have resisted the temptation to corrupt the optimal business design by trying to serve more than one target segment with their respective products.

Airline planners and analysts at conventional airlines are correct to continue using this fundamental analytical framework, but the conclusions they draw from their analyses and the outcomes they recommend must be dramatically different than in the past. The basic premise of this book is that the marketplace has changed so profoundly that the airline industry's traditional incremental approach to change is out-dated, preventing the sweeping changes in business design that are required to remain competitive and viable. Nothing short of radical new interpretations of results and their implications for whole new business designs are enough to save legacy conventional airlines.

The large conventional airlines have long recognized that they simultaneously serve many different market segments consisting of an extremely diverse customer base. However, obsessed with short term stock performance and market share as well as lack of management time and Board Room priorities, many of the struggling conventional airlines have ignored the implications of this basic marketing premise and clung to the antiquated one-size-fits-all strategy based on hub-and-spoke networks, multiple-class cabins, large and diverse fleets, complex pricing structures, and operations-driven service.

Over recent years, some conventional airlines in North America and Europe have attempted to operate low fare subsidiaries (Air Canada's Tango and Zip, British Airways' GO, Continental's Lite, Delta's Express, KLM's Buzz, SAS' Snowflake, United's Shuttle, US Airways' MetroJet, and so forth). Most failed because of poor implementation and a poor understanding of the market and passengers they were trying to serve. More recently, Delta's low fare operation, Song, appears to offer a superior product to its mainline service. It is important to note that the past failures do not mean the model is flawed, but rather suggest the execution of the model was flawed. The business model of separate independent subsidiaries remains viable, and many successful airlines will re-design their operations into highly specialized subsidiaries whose sole purpose is to serve a specific customer segment. For example, British Airways' subsidiary Go was not unsuccessful in the traditional sense. It was sold because it did not provide a strategic fit and possibly because it distracted the parent company making cost cuts at the mainline. It was clearly a success for its new owners (3i) who in turn sold it for a handsome price to easyJet. Consequently, unlike previous airline-within-airline operations, the new subsidiaries probably will be stand-alone operations, with unique and independent cultures, tactics, strategies and focus with a Southwest-like commitment to serving a single target segment.

Segmentation Strategies

Here are some examples of segmentation approaches that are being explored for conventional airlines and unconventional airlines:

- Air New Zealand's strategy has been nothing short of a rigorous restructuring of its core business rather than implementing incremental changes at the edges. The segmentation is clearly based on four very distinct markets, each requiring a very different strategy: domestic New Zealand; the Tasman between New Zealand and Australia; the South Pacific islands; and the long haul intercontinental routes to Asia, Europe, and North America. Air New Zealand is restructuring separately in each of these markets in recognition of the differences between them and the people they serve.

- British Airways' strategy is to be a global player, with a good balance between point-to-point and connecting traffic. The focus is clearly on business passengers travelling at premium fares, a strategy that requires constant innovation, exemplified by being the first to introduce beds in first and business classes. On the network side, the airline is clearly balancing its routes by reducing short haul services within Europe, and increasing long haul services to Africa and the Asia-Pacific region to reduce the high level of dependency on services in transatlantic markets. On the cost side, the focus is on simplification, centralization, and standardization.[2] Examples relate to such areas as fleet, maintenance and IT. For instance, since almost every business decision involves the availability of timely information, one of the first tasks was to centralize all information regarding all aspects of operations and customers.[3] Another part of the strategy relating to customers deals with making it easy for customers to do business with British Airways. The idea behind the "CeBA" concept (Customer-enabled BA) is to reduce as much as possible the human interaction in anything but face-to-face front line operations. This strategy provides customers with an option to serve themselves.[4]

- The shuttles operating in the US northeast region, operated now by Delta and US Airways, are long-standing examples of the type of focused business design that must be applied more broadly.

- Southwest and easyJet successfully target leisure travelers, and small business owners who buy tickets out of their own pockets. For the leisure traveler, the value position is simply a low price. For the frugal business traveler, it is frequent service to conventional airports at prices well below conventional business fares.

- Emirates (until recently a relatively small network carrier based in Dubai) has targeted the global marketplace—similar to Lufthansa and Virgin Atlantic (described below) but with one major difference. Whereas Lufthansa and Virgin are based in countries with a large O&D traffic base, Emirates relies almost completely on connecting traffic.

Consequently, Emirates has targeted numerous segments of the global market (ranging from the North American and European passengers traveling to the Middle East and Asia to Europeans traveling to the Pacific and virtually the entire Indian sub-Continent market) to be served by its global network, its relatively low costs, its excellent geographic location and its well-branded services. Although the strategy is similar to the one described below for Singapore, Singapore has certainly benefited from the fact that in many markets a passenger must make a stop for technical-operational reasons.

- Lufthansa has decided to pursue global markets given that it is based in the largest country in Europe and the home of some of the largest corporations in the world. Given the geographic spread of the population and location of business within Germany, Lufthansa's segmentation has led to the development of unique subsidiaries to serve the needs of its different segments. Business travelers out of second-tier German cities have services on all business class configured aircraft operating on a nonstop basis. First class passengers have a dedicated processing terminal at Frankfurt Airport. Premium class passengers making connections in Munich have access from almost 1,000 airports within Europe on corporate aircraft.

- Ryanair's strategy has been to focus on the ultra price conscious traveler. It is interesting to note that Ryanair's fare strategy has been so successful in penetrating its targeted segment that some people living in the UK have purchased property in other countries and based their personal lives around the existence of a Ryanair route.[5] In order to meet the needs of its targeted segments, Ryanair keeps its costs low by, among many other things, serving secondary/tertiary airports. Ryanair's experience has proven that some passengers will travel long distances to take advantage of the extremely low fare flights. For example, when Ryanair started service from Friedrichshafen, Germany to the UK, it was assumed that passengers would consist mostly of British people who had vacation homes in the area. Surprisingly, research showed that there were passengers from Austria, Switzerland and Italy, who had traveled many hours in their cars to take advantage of the very low fare service.[6]

- Singapore Airlines, having no domestic markets, decided, from the beginning, to serve a very broad spectrum of long haul international and intercontinental markets. Singapore Airlines developed a world renowned brand based on innovation and passenger services, exemplified by being a leader in operating a young fleet, developing state-of-the-art in-flight entertainment, and being the first carrier to operate in long haul markets—Singapore London and Singapore Los Angeles. The passenger segmentation was clearly balanced around core competencies, markets, and customers (being based half way between Europe and Australia. Clearly, customers prefer to travel nonstop, particularly those on business travel. Long haul travel, on the other hand, clearly requires the latest equipment and creature comforts—demonstrated core competencies of Singapore airlines. Finally, given the restricted nature of bilateral agreements with countries where Singapore Airlines made intermediate stops. Singapore needed to fly nonstop. For example, when the airline stopped in Tokyo before reaching Los Angeles, the Japanese placed restrictions on its operations. Consequently, the recently inaugurated nonstop flight enables Singapore Airlines to capitalize on the open skies policy with the US.

- Virgin Atlantic has focused on the intercontinental O&D segments from the UK (given the slot constraints at both airports). To meet the needs of this segment, Virgin has not only decided to serve the top O&D markets out of the top two UK airports but also offer unique products. Its well-branded Upper Class service priced at business class fares competes with some of the top brands' first class service. In addition, the carrier offers a premium economy product that is attractive to price conscious travelers on business or the more upscale travelers in the economy class. To penetrate the targeted segment, Virgin has developed other unique product features, both on the ground as well as in the cabin. Although, Virgin, Singapore and Emirates have strategies relating to high level brands, Virgin is clearly different from the other two. Virgin is carving out a niche in very large point-to-point markets with a "sexy/cool" product line. Such a strategy can work in a very unique base such as London. Even if only a small percentage of the market is attracted to such a product line, the absolute size of the traffic base is large enough to fill even the largest airplane on a daily basis.

These examples demonstrate that there is no one right way of attacking the marketplace. Segmentation strategies should be unique to the airline and reflect the specific and local conditions it faces in terms of geography, demography, regulatory framework, fleet, and the targeted customer base.

Optimizing Fleet for Flexibility and Customer Value

Most, although by no means all, drivers do not care how or where their cars are made. They are interested only in one thing—for the price paid does the car deliver what the driver is looking for? Similarly, many passengers (again, by no means, all) do not know, and do not care, about the jet aircraft they are flying on—even some experienced passengers are neither aware of, nor want to know, even the basics of the aircraft they are flying (manufacturer, age, number of engines and so forth). Passengers assume that aircraft are properly maintained and will be operated safely.

At many airlines, fleet planning has focused on operational and financial priorities, but in a customer-driven marketplace, airlines must radically rethink their entire fleet strategy, by focusing on how fleet decisions provide value for the passenger. Conventional airlines must give up the notion of expanding fleets to carry everyone to everywhere. There are too many strong niche airlines stealing shares in significant market segments. Consequently, successful airlines will focus their resources, including fleet, on specific targets and become more flexible in their competitive responses.

Airlines have long recognized that, like other capital-intensive industries, they must manage expensive capacity in the face of cyclical demand and rapidly changing competitive developments. The cycles in demand range from very short term peak/off-peak variations during the day to long term structural fluctuations associated with economic cycles. In addition, the well-publicized success of a few unconventional airlines (easyJet, Gol, Jet Airways, jetBlue, WestJet, Virgin Blue and so forth) has enabled the unconventional airlines to access capital to continue their rapid growth, which exacerbates the industry's chronic problem of mismatching supply and demand.

To prosper in the new customer-driven marketplace, successful airlines will adapt new fleet strategies that balance their customers' needs with the economic necessity of managing airline capacity and demand. In this environment, fleet planning at conventional airlines will be driven by the need for greater flexibility, which is the result of two contradictory forces at work in the industry. On the one hand, the weakened financial condition of many conventional airlines means they cannot afford to own and operate surplus capacity. On the other hand, conventional airlines cannot afford to have insufficient capacity during the brief periods of strong demand. In the former case of too much capacity, conventional airlines without the flexibility to reduce capacity often resort to marginal cost pricing to generate cash and fill seats, resulting in prolonged fare wars and operating losses. In the latter case of insufficient capacity, conventional airlines without the flexibility to add capacity incur a huge opportunity cost and loss of market share by not having sufficient capacity to take advantage of upswings in demand. Wet leasing may be part of the solution.

It has been argued that successful airlines will radically overhaul their business design by (a) divesting unprofitable markets and assets and (b) focusing remaining resources on smaller, but profitable target segments. An essential element of this dramatic restructuring is an entire realignment of the fleet. The optimal business design will reflect new thinking regarding the size, type and funding of the fleet. An airline could use wet leases to do development flying before committing its own fleet to a new market. Many conventional airlines today are burdened with inflexible contracts that limit their ability to adjust capacity to react to market developments.

Given the tremendous variability in demand and the changes in the competitive landscape, conventional airlines must reinvent themselves so that they can afford to pay for flexibility in managing capacity. By divesting losing business components and focusing on the optimal target markets, conventional airlines will be able to reposition their business focus, improve their capital structures and have the discipline and resources to pursue an effective fleet strategy. In the customer-driven marketplace, the primary components of an effective fleet strategy must include:

- Passenger focus—invest only in features that improve the passenger's life and for which passengers are willing to pay for (in excess of the costs of providing the features).

- Financing mix—gain flexibility to manage capacity in line with cyclical demand.

- Fleet mix—manage tradeoff of costly sub-fleets and the opportunity cost of not serving markets.

- Alliances—use alliances as surrogate fleet to serve target markets.

- Fleet age—design for short term retirement capability of part of capacity by using some older written-off airplanes (coupled with flexible capacity work rules).

Customer Focus

Customer focus means adding features only if it makes the customers' life better. For years, competing agendas of organizations within the typical conventional airline resulted in highly customized aircraft, which the manufacturers felt compelled to provide. For example, catering departments would demand large galleys and aisles, operating departments would demand engines, flight decks and maintenance procedures compatible with existing fleet types, and network planners would insist on payload-range options to serve new markets.

Although airlines may find customization appealing, there is a huge cost associated with customization. The manufacturers are not able to take full advantage of economies of scale and must raise their prices to cover the higher costs of customization. Moreover, customized aircraft have lower residual values and limit airline options when trying to dispose of unwanted capacity. By demanding customization, airlines pay more at delivery and receive less at the end of an aircraft's economic life cycle. In the new customer-driven marketplace, the only options airlines should be demanding from manufacturers, and be willing to pay for, are features that passengers will pay for and value. Fleet customization is one area where complexity is not justified—passengers are largely indifferent to the technical components (engines, avionics and so forth) and certain aspects of cabin configuration (the location of lavatories, galleys and so forth) of the aircraft they fly.

Financing Mix

Just as reducing the degree of customization will increase an airline's flexibility when adding or disposing of capacity, conventional airlines of the future must have more flexibility to manage their capacity in line with cyclical demand patterns. The optimal business design requires a financing mix that greatly enhances the airline's ability to add and subtract capacity as opportunities and threats arise. To improve flexibility, each airline's optimal business design will have an optimal financing mix of owned and leased aircraft, with a variety of maturity dates for the lease contracts.

The optimal financing mix will vary by airline, and by operating subsidiary for airlines pursuing more than one target market, based on the dynamics of the target markets. For example, an airline targeting a mature, business oriented market may find that the optimal financing mix is along of the lines of 60 percent owned, 25 percent leased on a long term basis and 15 percent on short term leases (ranging from 6-month to 24-month terms). On the other hand, an airline whose business strategy focuses on entering new markets to attract price sensitive discretionary travelers may need a more flexible financing mix to adapt swiftly to changes in seasonal demand patterns—for example, 40 percent of the fleet owned, 30 percent on long term leases and 40 percent on short term leases.

The objective is to lock up the appropriate portion of the fleet at favorable long term rates, which will provide a stable foundation for long term growth. In addition, as owned aircraft become fully funded, they can be grounded at minimal cost in the event of sudden demand fluctuations. On the other hand, having a large number of aircraft on lease provides some additional flexibility and ways to manage risky developments, albeit at a higher cost as the lessor will demand higher rates for assuming some of the risk of return. Nevertheless, conventional airlines must have the flexibility to change capacity quickly in the new customer-driven marketplace. To that end, successful airlines with sufficient financial resources may be able to negotiate put and call options with lessors to return and accept aircraft on relatively short notice. Moreover, there is a need for innovative financing that provides for "walk-away leases".

Of course, such flexibility comes at a cost. Providers of credit will require higher rates due to the uncertainty of airline demands. Moreover, airline planners will be under even greater pressure to forecast correctly and management must have the discipline to accept and reject capacity on a regular basis as dictated by market conditions. In addition, managing crew resources will be much more difficult, which will require greater cooperation and coordination between management and labor (particularly in situations involving wet leases).

However, more than offsetting these costs is the ability to swiftly shift capacity—a relatively easy task once airplanes are standardized—to meet changing market conditions, which will greatly enhance the long term viability and competitiveness of a passenger-focused conventional airline. A conventional airline's investment in revenue management systems will be optimized, and financial performance improved, if the airline can minimize the time and cost of adding and deleting capacity in response to cyclical patterns of demand. The industry's inability to match demand and capacity is the single largest contributor to ruinous fare wars and the conventional airlines' inability to generate sustainable economic returns. Developing a radical new business design that optimizes fleet flexibility will help conventional airlines achieve much better long term profits.

Fleet Mix

How Many Fleet Types? Another contributor to the conventional airlines' current problems is the number of sub-fleets, which have been acquired over the years in the misguided quest to take everyone to everywhere. Conventional airlines are beginning to realize that the huge investment in large and diverse fleets has limited their ability to make competitive responses, exemplified by the experience of SAS. Having tied their financial resources in fleets that were built in a different era to serve a much different marketplace, conventional airlines now lack the financial resources to quickly change their fleet mix. Conventional airlines are struggling because they lack sufficient aircraft of the right type to compete with the unconventional airlines, while also maintaining a strong competitive presence in strategic core markets. In contrast to the complex fleets of conventional airlines, unconventional airlines have been able to build their fleets based on serving a single target customer segment. By limiting their fleet to a single type with the right payload-range performance and the optimal cost structure to serve the marketplace, the unconventional airlines have been able to divert traffic from the conventional airlines.

Many conventional airlines have come to realize the enormous costs of maintaining too many sub-fleets. American, for example, has reduced its fleet types from 14 down to six. Aer Lingus has been moving toward not just two types—the 330s and 320s—but with no variations even within a single type, relying on only the 320 and not 319 or 321. Reducing sub-fleets does result in cost savings—training, maintenance, specialized ground equipment, and so forth—but more importantly, the reduced sub-fleet, in conjunction with a disciplined focus on specific target markets, makes the airline a more nimble and effective competitor. In the customer-driven marketplace, the configuration and range requirements of an airline's fleet are now dictated by the value demands of the targeted customer segments, and will vary according to each airline's optimal business design. In this light, however, it is possible with care to leverage the diversity in fleet to achieve superior competitive responses. Assuming that the airline has in place the relevant processes, the mindset, the discipline, and labor cooperation, an airline can play almost in real time the supply-demand balancing game. Contrast this with an airline with one type of an aircraft who can only play the supply-demand balancing game with one weapon—price.

Targeting the Right Segment   Those airlines that have the resources and ability to operate several different subsidiaries serving unique segments will require more sub-fleets than an airline targeting only one customer segment. The complexity of targeted networks would determine the optimal number of sub-fleets. For example, Virgin Atlantic's business model focuses on serving the largest long haul markets from London Heathrow and Gatwick, which include a mix of business and leisure destinations. As a result, Virgin's optimal fleet mix will include basically two different cabin configurations reflecting the different value expectations in each market. Passenger expectations in the Heathrow-US markets are different from the expectations of passengers in the Gatwick-Caribbean markets. Therefore, 747s flying from Heathrow have different configurations than those flying from Gatwick.

On the other hand, an airline choosing to target a price sensitive market may opt for a single cabin configuration, which greatly reduces operational complexity. With just one aircraft type the airline can save money because all aircraft can be staffed and provisioned in the same way. Moreover, a single aircraft type can optimize revenue management, especially in the event of irregular operations. If a flight has to be canceled, airlines with a single fleet type can roll out a replacement plane that will immediately re-accommodate all passengers. This would be a huge advantage in having, for example, only one type of aircraft in the single aisle category for the targeted market—especially for a small airline. Cancellations for airlines with several fleet types typically result in suboptimal solutions as the airline is forced to replace the canceled flight with another airplane of a different size—a replacement that is too small incurs denied boarding charges and a replacement that is too big incurs unnecessary operating costs. In addition to having to use different sized aircraft to handle irregular operations, airlines with multiple fleets also struggle to match crews with available aircraft during irregular operations. Airlines with a single fleet type save costs by having all reserve pilots qualified to fly all spare aircraft, thereby minimizing customer inconvenience and airline costs during irregular operations. Again, the decision on aircraft is tied very closely to the decision on the market to be served and the degree of complexity desired, such as an analysis of spill and recapture of revenues.

Planning the Right Fleet Mix Unconventional airlines, such as Southwest and Ryanair, who target discretionary travelers, have long recognized that they can minimize costs and complexity by having a single fleet type (even though, strictly speaking, Southwest has two types, the older 737 is quite different from the newer 737 in such areas as cockpits and technology). On the other hand, some conventional airlines have developed new business plans that seek to attract more than just price sensitive passengers in domestic markets. As a result, these conventional airlines have reduced their fleets to reduce costs and to better serve those target segments. As mentioned above, American reduced its fleet from 14 types down to six. For American to reduce further would probably incur a substantial opportunity cost as the airline would be unable to serve desirable target markets.

The optimal fleet mix for Southwest and jetBlue is obviously much different than the optimal fleet mix for American. But in all cases, the optimal mix is driven by the airline's business strategy to appeal to specific target segments. Southwest has, up to now, stuck with one fleet type to minimize costs and complexity, even though that strategy means the airline cannot serve some markets. jetBlue, on the other hand, has decided to enter thinner markets with a fleet of aircraft with 100 seats. A quick analysis of O&D markets in the US shows hundreds of markets that are underserved and or overpriced and that can be served economically with a new generation of regional jets. At the other end of the spectrum, an airline like American accepts the costs of operating a more complex fleet as its focus is on serving more market segments. It will be interesting to see how the unconventional airlines are able to deal with two types of airplanes and maintain low costs. jetBlue in the USA and easyJet in Europe have both ordered a second type of aircraft in their fleets. Assuming that both airlines negotiated extremely attractive financial packages with the manufacturers and assuming that both airlines identified appropriate markets, there is no reason that the airlines would not be able to maintain their cost leadership.

A recent example of a major re-fleeting exercise is Air Canada. In April 2005, the airline announced the complete replacement of its wide body fleet—a total of 71 aircraft, to take place over a 10 year period. The current 767 fleet had two different engines, resulting from the consolidation with Canadian International. Having the same aircraft with two different engines types is almost as expensive as having two different airframes, due to maintenance, spares, training, and crew costs. In that context, Air Canada's decision actually cuts its wide body fleet types not from six to two but from seven to two. With a two class capacity in the current active fleet ranging from 198 in the 767-200 to 282 in the 340-300, there were a lot of different aircraft types covering a relatively small range in capacity.[7]

The replacement aircraft are a mixture of the 777 and the 787 with a capacity range from about 223 to about 368 seats—a wider range than the aircraft they replace and accomplished with only two types. This strategy will compliment Air Canada's single aisle fleet commonality of the 320 series and greatly simplify scheduling, maintenance, training, crew and irregular operations. The strategy will also provide improved operating economics, wide payload range and attractive interiors for passengers. This market positioning with mid-size wide bodies will allow the build-up of frequencies in thin emerging markets in South America and the Asia Pacific region, particularly China which recently signed a new bilateral with Canada.

In the final analyses, successful fleet management in the new marketplace is driven by two fundamental questions.

- How do I improve my flexibility to manage the supply-demand equation?

- Does my investment in fleet resources enhance the target customer's value?

A lot of airline executives used to think that passengers would not accept smaller aircraft on long haul routes. However, as discussed in the next chapter, Continental's extensive experience with trans-Atlantic service with the 757 and a number of regional jet flight legs approaching four hours are making airline executives rethink their positions. Ultimately, if these trends are extrapolated, the potential exists for small, long haul jets that serve transcontinental and trans-Atlantic markets.

Alliances

Fleet Simplification through Partnering For many airlines, there are more market opportunities than aircraft of the right number and type. In the past, that meant airlines either chose not to serve those markets or acquired costly sub-fleets to serve a limited number of markets. The competitive marketplace requires airlines to take advantage of all opportunities, in the most efficient manner, and the advent of alliances presents conventional airlines an opportunity to do just that.

When an airline identifies a market it really wants to serve, the next question is whether the airline has the necessary resources—route authority, fleet, airport staff and local marketing expertise—to serve the market profitably. If not, alliance partners may provide a viable substitute. In addition, airlines with considerable alliance experience have learned they can optimize fleet assignments across each other's networks. For example, one airline with a fleet of 767 aircraft can coordinate schedules with an alliance partner who operates a fleet of 330 aircraft so that each aircraft type optimally serves the right market. In this way, savvy airlines are substituting alliance resources for expensive investments in fleet. For example, most airlines have few routes where they can deploy economically the new ultra long haul aircraft. Serving these segments through alliances could be an extremely cost effective strategy. Singapore and Thai Airways have already begun a nonstop service with the 340-500 across the Pacific. One would assume that mutually beneficial code-sharing arrangements could be made for service to United's hubs in San Francisco and Chicago's O'Hare.

Increasing the Market Impact   Serving segments of the market through an alliance partner certainly has many advantages such as market enlargement, and a diversified portfolio to maximize geographic coverage at the least cost. However, serving a segment through an alliance partner also has some risks. The most important types of risks include the possibility of customer confusion, erosion of image in some cases and employee resistance. See Chapter 7 for more detail. Whether the airline joins a multilateral or one or more bilateral alliances to serve the targeted segment(s) would depend heavily on the nature of the segment(s)—type, number, geographic location, as well as market characteristics such as density, traffic mix, seasonality and directionality. Lufthansa, for example, does not serve Australia despite being a global player. It serves the market through its partners—Singapore and Thai Airways—in the multilateral alliance (Star). Japan Airlines, on the other hand, is not a member of a multilateral alliance, but instead has separate and varying agreements with many airlines worldwide. The decision whether to join a multilateral alliance is complex. See Chapter 7 for a detailed discussion of the pros and cons of alliance membership.

In summary, airlines must redesign their entire network to focus on the limited number of target segments that offer the best financial returns given the airline's competitive strengths. All network, fleet, and alliance partnerships that do not provide value to the targeted segment(s) must be divested so that the airline can focus all remaining resources on becoming a dominant force in the target market. This radical redesign requires the airline to strategically align its fleet—including financing mix and types—and alliances with the new network and target market. If, for example, the optimal business design warrants the use of alliances as a viable substitute for costly investments in new routes or fleet types, the airline should put aside its ego and work with labor to maximize the value provided to the customer.

Aligning the Corporate Culture

Fighting the Last War

To accomplish the segmentation, fleet composition and alliance partnership steps outlined above requires a major change in culture. Unfortunately, the inability to change corporate culture may well be the biggest obstacle for conventional airlines to develop strategies that move them beyond survivability and short term staying power to profitable growth in the long term.

Generals are often criticized for fighting the last war—using old and outdated strategies and tactics. Each new war presents entirely new enemies, weapons and tactics, and requires different strategies to win. Airline strategies and tactics that worked in the early years after deregulation are no longer appropriate. For example, airlines need to do away with thinking that the FFP is the only way to build loyalty from everyone. In the future, in most markets, the best way to build loyalty will be by delivering what the passenger really wants when buying an airline ticket—consistent, reliable, hassle free and predictable transportation, at a fair price. Similarly airlines cannot continue to rely on fortress hubs to protect them from nimble competitors. Airline executives, like generals, cannot win today's battles with yesterday's tactics.

Given the pace and severity of changes sweeping the industry, many carriers are struggling with what to do:

- Resort to old-fashioned remedies and hope that they produce different results; or

- Radically redesign the entire business.

For many executives, the first option is appealing. Adopting old remedies that once worked—grounding aircraft and canceling orders, furloughing employees and cutting benefits, canceling flights, altering distribution strategies, reducing onboard amenities, slashing fares to generate cash flow, and so forth—enable management to demonstrate a plan of action. Skeptics who question management's adoption of old remedies are reminded that the old remedies have enabled conventional airlines to survive prior downturns. Management strives to convince skeptics that the old remedies will work again if given enough time. Of course, the focus on cost reduction does provide a temporary financial benefit; the cost cuts will reduce the size of operating losses in the short term. Unfortunately, airline executives who rely on old style remedies have the same mindset as generals fighting the last war—they are hoping that history will repeat itself. They have deluded themselves into believing that it is possible, even likely, that passenger revenue will recover to the exuberant levels of the dotcom era, and that the surviving conventional airlines will be able to reassert their pricing power and return to profitability.

The perception of value in air travel has forever been reset in the minds of passengers. What makes up value has changed. Consumers are now empowered to shop until they find value. Moreover, in the absence of the liquidation of several large conventional airlines, demand will have to grow at high rates if the equilibrium price of supply and demand is ever to be significantly enhanced.

The Changing Competitive Landscape

The rapid growth of the unconventional airlines will continue to introduce capacity to the industry, some for new, under- or non-served markets and some to serve the freshly stimulated demand. Either way, the new capacity will exert downward pressure on fares. For example, in the US, four unconventional airlines (AirTran, America West[8], jetBlue and Southwest) have orders for delivery of 300 aircraft in the next four years. The incremental aircraft being added by these four unconventional airlines is equivalent to the fleet now operated by Continental. Not only are the unconventional airlines adding the equivalent of a major airline to an industry already suffering from overcapacity, but the incremental capacity will be introduced at unconventional airline cost rates. The situation is similar in Europe. The two largest unconventional airlines, easyJet and Ryanair, are both expected to add a new aircraft approximately every two weeks until the end of 2008.[9]

Given the continuing competitive pressure the unconventional airlines will exert, and the changing demands of customers, it seems very unlikely that the old remedies of the past will prove effective in the current environment. Rather than rely on the remedies of the past to solve current problems, management of any airline must view their competitive position in radically different ways. An integral component of the new thinking is to change one's corporate culture to make the airline more flexible, passenger focused and disciplined. Moreover, the imperative for change in corporate culture may not apply to just conventional airlines, but also to some unconventional airlines.

The problems of conventional airlines have provided easy-pickings for the unconventional airlines, and capturing share from the over priced, insensitive, lethargic conventional airlines has been relatively easy. By offering a very appealing alternative to conventional airlines, the unconventional airlines have both stimulated demand and shifted demand from the conventional airlines. Moreover, there are still many markets with pent-up demand, such as to and from the Paris area and from former Eastern Europe, implying that competitive pressures on conventional airlines will not abate soon. Although conventional airlines have the most urgent need for change, unconventional airlines must also be alert to shifting market conditions. Some research shows that of the traffic transported by unconventional airlines within Europe, about three-quarters was stimulated traffic and about one-fourth diverted from the incumbent airlines.[10] If one assumes that most of the pent-up demand has already been satisfied (true for markets such as the UK, Ireland, Belgium and some German cities), then as the unconventional airlines continue to grow, it is inevitable that they will begin to compete more aggressively with the conventional airlines as well as with each other, resulting in the need to sharpen their strategic focus and maintain tighter discipline. Moreover, growth also can mean higher costs as inefficiencies creep into an unconventional airline's operations and management's attention is spread over a more diverse base.

Requirements on Management

The formulation of a productive corporate culture is as important to the unconventional airlines as it is to the conventional airlines. The unconventional airlines must ensure that the corporate culture that fueled the company's growth is sustained as their airlines grow and large numbers of new employees join the workforce. On the other hand, conventional airlines are challenged to adopt and foster a corporate culture that is consistent with their optimal new business design. Although the challenges are different—the unconventional airlines strive to maintain a successful culture, while the conventional airlines struggle to implement new ones—the basic requirements on management are the same. They include accountability for:

- Change.

- Strategic Focus.

- Implementation.

- Corporate Performance.

- Labor Relations.

Accountability for Change   Managements are paid for developing a strategic vision, and in the current environment that means seeing new ways of seeing—going beyond conventional wisdom. For many conventional airlines, the time has come to leap beyond incremental change, and to completely overhaul the airline's network, fleet, product, pricing, distribution and business strategy. Management must give up the "me-too" approach to change in the industry, where the major airlines copy each other and they all end up offering indistinguishable service. Managements of conventional airlines must discard their traditional arrogance regarding the unconventional airlines' ability to serve premier routes. Many conventional airlines had argued that the products and services offered by short haul unconventional airlines would preclude them from becoming effective competitors in the domestic transcontinental markets. The success of jetBlue and Southwest has clearly disproved that argument. Some conventional airlines continue to believe that unconventional airlines will never be able to significantly penetrate intercontinental routes, because such routes are inherently different and customers will only accept what the conventional airlines have to offer. Delta, though, has taken the opposite approach, switching its transcontinental flights from conventional two-class mainline service over to its low-cost, one-class Song division. The question remains are the conventional airlines correct about the unconventional airlines inability to penetrate intercontinental routes? It is worth noting that the success of the unconventional airlines is due to their ability to consistently impress on "targeted" passengers that they are offering something different—consistent, reliable, friendly service at a fair price on an everyday basis. In this context, only a few conventional airlines have succeeded.

Accountability for Strategic Focus   Managements at many conventional airlines must give up the idea of trying to be all-purpose airlines. The misguided and discredited market share mentality, which fueled conventional airlines' growth for years, is no longer valid. The pursuit of market share, without regard for the airline's core customer base or profitability, has resulted in the mismanagement of scarce resources and diverted attention from the manageable number of strategies and tactics that could ensure the airline's long term future. The airline industry has become highly segmented, as a variety of unconventional airlines are now serving profitable niches that used to be key conventional airline segments. To remain viable, conventional airlines must similarly limit their focus to targeted segments and have the discipline to forgo unprofitable segments. In so doing, managements will be better able to identify and focus on competition and to deliver valued customer service.

Accountability for Implementation   Developing a grand new strategy is easy—the really hard work is recognizing and solving all of the problems inherent in the details of implementing a new strategy. Many of the best strategies have failed because management would rather focus on grand strategy than be bothered with the tedium of implementation. Management must devote the same level of energy, resources and attention to implementation as it does to strategy formulation. In some cases, senior executives do not posses the necessary skills to achieve effective implementation of strategy. In some cases, the implementation phase does not carry the pizzazz that comes with strategy development and, as such, implementation tends to be handed down to the new person in the group or some junior staff member. In the new environment, senior management must see the forest and the trees—the big picture (that is, the need to completely rethink the optimal business design) and the details of implementation. For example, low-cost subsidiaries are appropriate strategies—if, and only if, they are properly implemented and managed. The enormous consequence of not placing sufficient focus on implementation is a failed strategy. The subsequent loss of corporate resources and the further deterioration in customer perceptions allow competitors to become more entrenched. See Chapter 8 for further comments on implementation and execution.

Accountability for Corporate Performance   Airlines, like all large businesses suffer from a "silo" mentality, where each department focuses on its performance without regard for the overall good of the business. Departments who demand resources—maintenance taking aircraft out of service, crew scheduling rejecting efficient aircraft rotations, sales promising new business if new flights are added, customer loyalty developing reward programs that compromise revenue management—must develop sound business cases to justify the requested resources, track the financial performance of their actions and be held accountable for the actual performance. In addition to the "silo" problem, there is an equally harmful problem that some business analysts refer to as "turf battles" or fiefdoms".[11] Here executives in charge of their departments try to—intentionally or unintentionally—protect their turf by controlling resources or information, or using "complexity of their operations" as a reason to not have to justify their decisions. At some airlines, for example, the maintenance, engineering and technical operations department is viewed as a "black box". Marketing and finance find it difficult to question the resources requested or the processes implemented.

Accountability for Labor Relations   Despite the huge investments in capital assets and technology, airlines have huge investments in their labor to deliver the services that passengers value. In general, successful airlines have a reputation for productive, motivated and service oriented employees. Fostering a successful corporate culture requires better labor management relations. Executives who negotiate labor agreements cannot use labor as an excuse for poor financial performance. To build trust and credibility with labor and customers, executives cannot use airline's assets as resources for personal enrichment—rewarding themselves with huge bonuses while demanding sacrifices from labor.

In addition, productive labor relations require openness and honesty in communications up and down the chain of command and between departments. By fostering honest communications, senior management will reduce distrust between labor and management, and minimize internal rivalries between departments. Management's effectiveness ultimately depends on lower level employees successfully implementing strategies. The enthusiasm and dedication employees have for following management's grand vision is driven by the trust that employees have in management. The level of trust that employees have in management is determined by the effectiveness, candor and honesty of communication between employee groups.

Much has been written about the success of unconventional airlines in general and Southwest in particular. Although the list of critical success factors includes the achievement of low costs through such factors as the simplicity of products and processes, corporate culture continues to be the center piece of the list. Here are just a couple of examples of what the top management at Southwest has preached and practiced. Herb Kelleher (Chairman) has been reported to say, "We don't take ourselves too seriously". And that there is little tolerance for managers who do not practice corporate humility or who go on ego trips. In an interview Jim Parker (President) is quoted as describing the following situation at a bargaining table with organized labor. While both sides can be tough with one another, both sides want the best for the customer and Southwest Airlines.[12]

Conclusions

The airline industry appears to be evolving towards the segmented structure that existed prior to deregulation—a small number of large trunk carriers offering long haul domestic and intercontinental services, regional carriers offering short and medium haul services within geographic areas and commuter carriers offering very short haul services to small communities. In aviation's formative years, this structure was developed and controlled by government regulators. However, today's evolution toward the segmented marketplace is being driven and controlled by market forces with low entry barriers.

Recognition that the optimal structure of the aviation industry is a segmented market with specialized carriers means that it is not possible for one airline to efficiently serve all segments with an undifferentiated product. Indeed, the unconventional airlines and regional jet operators are succeeding because their operations, marketing programs and business strategies are optimally designed to serve one defined segment. The conventional airlines are struggling because their one-size-fits-all operations, marketing programs and business strategies are not a good fit for the segments they try to serve, and the unconventional airlines are able to attack the conventional airlines by offering services that are specialized to the market segment.

The current environment has already proven to be turbulent. The emerging environment is expected to be much more uncertain. Consequently, both types of airlines are vulnerable. The conventional airlines have certainly worked hard to reduce costs, simplify operations and revitalize products. Unfortunately, as one business analyst points out, many organizations continue to be vulnerable as a result of ignorance, inflexibility, indifference and inconsistency. Sadly, this conclusion applies to many conventional airlines. On the positive side, according to the same business analyst with expertise in organizational performance, there are proven remedies for organizational vulnerability—alertness, agility, adaptability and alignment.[13] By trying to be all things to all passengers, many conventional airlines have satisfied only a few. To succeed in today's customer-driven marketplace, all airlines—although conventional more than unconventional—must properly segment and fragment the market, design products and services that provide real and lasting value to the targeted segment and adopt a corporate culture that promotes a highly disciplined focus on consistently delivering reliable service to the targeted customers. While the need to segment, target and position is not new, what is new are (a) the urgency with which conventional more than unconventional airlines must undertake rigid analyses of their markets, customers and core competencies, and (b) the discussions of how the results of the analyses must now be interpreted differently to radically overhaul their business designs.

Notes

[1] Binggeli, Urs and Lucio Pompeo, "The battle for Europe's low-fare flyers", *McKinsey on Travel & Logistics*, January 2005, pp. 1-7.

[2] Hurd, Mark and Lars Nyberg, *The Value Factor: How Global Leaders Use Information for Growth and Competitive Advantage* (Princeton, NJ: Bloomberg Press, 2004), p. 23.

[3] Hurd, Mark and Lars Nyberg, *The Value Factor: How Global Leaders Use Information for Growth and Competitive Advantage* (Princeton, NJ: Bloomberg Press, 2004), p. 49.

[4] "British Airways' CeBA vision", *Aviation Strategy*, June 2004, p. 17.

[5] "Battle of the slots", *Airline Fleet & Network Management*, January-February 2005, p. 53.

[6] "Battle of the slots", *Airline Fleet & Network Management*, January-February 2005, p. 54.

[7] ACE Aviation, "Widebody Fleet Order for Air Canada", An External Briefing Paper, April 25, 2005. Available on Air Canada's website.

[8] In Table 1.1 America West was shown as a conventional airline. It is now a born again unconventional airline.

[9] "The expansionist dilemma", *Aviation Strategy*, June 2004, p. 1.

[10] Binggeli, Urs and Lucio Pompeo, "The battle for Europe's low-fare flyers", *McKinsey on Travel & Logistics*, January 2005, p. 2.

[11] Herbold, Robert, *The Fifedom Syndrome: The Turf Battles that Undermine Carriers and Companies—and How to Overcome Them* (New York: Doubleday, 2004).

[12] Underwood, Jim, *What's Your Corporate IQ?: How the Smartest Companies Learn, Transform, Lead* (Chicago, IL: Dearborn Trade Publishing, 2004), pp. 133-139.

[13] Light, Paul C., *The Four Pillars of High Performance: How Robust Organizations Achieve Extraordinary Results* (New York: McGraw-Hill, 2005), pp. 4-16.

Chapter 4

Renovating and Innovating Products

Just as the previous chapter pointed out that by trying to be all things to all passengers, many conventional airlines have satisfied only a few, it can also be maintained that the current product portfolio of many conventional airlines is overly complex and in its complexity it misses the mark. It fails to provide adequate value for either the business segment or the VFR-leisure segment. This hypothesis is supported by the success of the business models of unconventional airlines worldwide and the expansion of fractional ownership in corporate aircraft and corporate shuttles. Consequently, conventional airlines, much more than unconventional airlines, need to revitalize old products and create new products to provide adequate value to the changing needs of the targeted customers.

In this chapter the definition of product is very broad. It covers the full continuum from network and schedule related features to cabin configurations and airport processes to brands and loyalty related features, to redesigning existing aircraft to meet specific passenger needs. During a product evaluation process, while possible for an airline to look to innovation, it may be more cost effective and realistic to aim for product renovation than innovation. There are two key considerations in considering renovation over innovation. First, it is more cost effective to renovate and revitalize existing products. An example of this would be introducing nonstop services in some markets and improving on time performance. Second, is renovation possible, or viable for some products? For example, has the first class product outlived its usefulness on many intercontinental markets just as it has within European markets where it is now called business class? The viability of renovation should be tied to changes in the marketplace, such as:

- The dynamic change in traffic mix, with the leisure-VFR segments growing at a much higher rate than the business segment.

- The entry of new competitors into existing markets, not just low-cost, low fare airlines, but also lower cost and high profile brand network airlines such as those based in the Middle East—Emirates.

- The availability of new aircraft technology such as ultra long haul airplanes (such as the 340-500 and the 777-200LR) at one end of the spectrum and long range, more comfortable regional jets and high speed turboprops at the other end of the spectrum.

- Combinations of products never offered before.

- The shift in the power relationship from scheduled airline to the passenger.

Revisiting Customer Concerns and Expectations

Many passengers prefer nonstop over connecting service. Some may prefer connecting service if it is accompanied by high frequency and does not involve severe penalties in total trip time. Some may not a have choice if they live in areas that generate insufficient traffic for nonstop service. Based on the degree of hub development over the past two decades, it is clear that conventional airlines preferred to transport passengers via hubs even in markets that could support nonstop service. Hubs enabled conventional airlines to consolidate traffic, deploy large aircraft with low unit operating costs, obtain premium yield from local traffic, use the breadth of destinations served to attract frequent flyers and corporate accounts and use the power of frequency to achieve superior status on computer reservation screens. Passengers, of course, had little choice until the unconventional airlines started nonstop services in markets.

Passengers prefer nonstop service even if it means smaller airplanes, for example regional jets in domestic markets and single aisles in international markets. There is evidence that passengers would be willing to fly four hours in regional jets or eight hours in single aisle jets if they could get to their destination substantially faster via a nonstop.

Passengers prefer to have greater visible differentiation for the variation in price in economy class cabins. Conventional airlines charge a wide range of prices for virtually the same product (as perceived by customers). The price differentiation was more a function of revenue management than visible product features. See the discussion on pricing policies in the next chapter. The fare logic worked backwards. It started with a very high "normal economy" fare and came down with each restriction. Would passengers have instead preferred to have a very low basic fare and then be allowed to purchase product features in incremental value? Business passengers, when they were paying extraordinary high fares, were not comfortable traveling with low fare paying leisure travelers in the same cabin. The later segment can cause delays. For example: The airport processing takes too long because infrequent travelers take longer to be processed. Departing aircraft are delayed due to the additional time required to get the plane ready for push back. Arriving aircraft are delayed when the deplaning process is too long due to more passengers and infrequent travelers who do not "know the ropes".[1]

Customers feel that there need to be more price-service options between the economy class and business class in intercontinental markets. A few airlines do offer such products such as British Airways, British Midland, EVA and Virgin Atlantic. In international markets, the difference between the Economy class and Business class price-service options is quite significant. Transatlantic passengers would love to be able to go in more comfort than being squeezed at the back if they could pay a little more, but not the difference between $800 and $5000. It would be a lot better than the 31 inches of seat pitch that they currently endure. People who buy premium class tickets feel they are entitled to special recognition— not only separate boarding and deplaning but also privacy.

From passengers' viewpoint loyalty programs need a careful reevaluation. The first generation of the frequent flyer program was introduced by American. The current programs need serious renovation. Some corporations even claim, for example, that some passengers take unnecessary trips to accumulate extra miles.[2] There is complexity—who gets the awards, the passenger or the company? What about their role in alliances? What is the cost of such programs? What is the balance between rewarding past travel and enticing future flyers? Passengers cannot redeem the miles for the itineraries of their choice. Seats are not available. The situation has become worse with an increase in load factors. The upgrades are a waste of time, at least in the US where they are given to people with higher status cards. It seems to some passengers that everyone else is a gold or an elite member. Does that possibly mean that airlines made it too easy to get that status? In Europe, airlines have been much more protective of their premium cabins and there are virtually no free upgrades, regardless of status. Finally, although alliances have provided consumers with more options for using frequent flyer miles, the complexity of the arrangement may just make consumers feel that it is not worth the effort to find out if they can use their Airline A miles on Airline B. Moreover, airline websites, for the most part, do not allow passengers to book partner award tickets online, forcing consumers to call the airline and pay a fee for the booking.

Passengers want to be recognized in ways other than free trips and upgrades and access to lounges. For example, take care of them when things go wrong. Suppose airline A's flight is late. Put the passenger on a competitor instead of making the passenger wait for an indefinite period until the unserviceable airplane is fixed. Airline A's delayed flight is an uncertainty. The competitor's flight is leaving now. Prompt caring actions from the viewpoint of the customer are a very powerful form of loyalty.

Finally, passengers are concerned about the basic elements of products. Passengers appear to be more concerned about the inconsistency in service than the lower level of service. They do not want surprises. Passengers want an improvement in the basic product, namely, on-time performance. Airlines say, for example, that their on-time performance is 80 percent. Customers see two problems with this. If a passenger misses the connection because of the delay in deplaning or the time required to get to a boarding gate, then it may be an on-time arrival from the viewpoint of the airline but not from the perspective of the customer. Moreover, 80 percent may sound high but a customer may look at that number and say, "this means to me that this is the equivalent of each and every plane being late one day in a work week", Next, some passengers are amazed how difficult it is to get any information from airlines during irregular operations, let alone accurate information. What message is given when it appears that no one is in charge?

Renovating Existing Products

Obviously ideal products are those that provide value for customers and profits for airlines. Unfortunately, many products have achieved neither objective. Consequently, the starting point for product renovation might be to list key objectives such as:

- Customer perceived value.

- Minimum complexity from the airline's and the passenger's perspectives but user friendly self service features that add value for the customer and the airline.

- Airline's ability to communicate clearly the value proposition relating to the product.

- A realistic understanding of market positioning.

- Revenue potential by getting existing customers to buy more or by getting new customers or both.

- Built in flexibility (for example, creating a business class in short and medium haul markets by simply restricting the sale of the middle seat).

Past problems relating to poor profitability of products have related to:

- Lack of adequate market research (for example, customers' expectations, perception of value, and ranking of priorities by type of customer and by the same customer at different times).

- Poor implementation (for example, premature introduction of business class products at some airlines, or announcing a new product after the decision to offer it is made, rather than on the implementation date).

- Poor pricing policies (for example, no options for passengers to make tradeoffs).

- Poor communications (building too high or too low expectations relative to performance).

- Lack of adequate meaningful product differentiation among competitors.

- Lack of information on product profitability, including the computation of product "loss leaders".

- Insufficient attention to improvements in basic product features (for example, reliability, correct and timely information).

- Too much focus on the needs of premium traffic, a segment that is not growing as rapidly as the more price sensitive segment.

- Lack of measurements on critical services, meaning if it is not measured, it will not be improved.

The renovation of existing products can be analyzed using an old technique. Although old, the Boston Box theory is still valuable for evaluating the product portfolio. The concept can be applied to many products—routes, cabin configurations, loyalty programs and so forth. The original idea discussed four categories—dogs, and stars along one direction, that is, if the market is not growing and the airline has a small share, give it up. It is a dog, such as first class service across the Atlantic for second and third tier airlines. Similarly for some airlines it could be a star if they have a very high market share of a high growth product—premium economy for Virgin, for example. The other categories are the cash cows and wildcats (sometimes called question marks).[3] Products are classified along two dimensions—market growth and market share. The big payoffs from renovation could be in the category of products where the market is growing but the airline has a small share, for example, premium traffic. An airline could introduce meaningful premium products. Stars are obviously worth protecting. Lufthansa's use of all business class airplanes is a perfect example. But that is also the area where competition is likely to be the most competitive.

A framework similar to the one discussed above could be used to analyze the cost effectiveness of fragmenting traffic out of a major city on high capacity airplanes versus transporting the traffic on smaller airplanes. For example, would it be cost effective for a major airline such as Air France, or British Airways, or Lufthansa to fly their first class passengers across the Atlantic in 10 first class seats in corporate jets, their business class passengers in 40 business class seats in single aisle jets, and their economy class passengers in 200, 300, or 400 economy class seats in twin aisle aircraft? Some experiments are already underway. Lufthansa and Air France, for example, are already offering service in selected markets with single aisle jets configured in all business classes.

The issue of fragmentation vs. consolidation is truly complex and there is no general answer. Obviously, customers want to go direct but they are not willing to pay the price. Based on numerous discussions with airline pricing executives, the three most important things to customers now-a-days are price, price and price. It is not just in economy class. Even the premium class passengers are looking at price. Of course, they are willing to pay varying amounts more for higher service cabins, but price is still very much in the picture.

The main consideration regarding separate aircraft depends on the type of airline, the traffic base, and the objectives. For example, what are the objectives of first class in intercontinental markets—profitability or brand image? Many airlines no longer offer first class across the Atlantic. Of those who still offer this product, some admit that it does not make a profit even at the exorbitantly high fares. The main reason for the loss is related to the extremely low load factor computed on a paying passenger basis (that is, excluding upgrades and airline staff). Even the airlines that still offer first class, do not offer it on all aircraft. Reasons for continuation of first class service vary from airline to airline. Some offer it for prestige and image reasons—the first class being the flag ship, the Maybach of Mercedes. Another reason may be that the aircraft is used on more than one intercontinental route. For example, a European airline flying across the Atlantic may use the same aircraft flying to the Middle East where there may be sufficient first class traffic. In fact, across the Atlantic, New York to London, Heathrow is probably the only market that can justify for a first class cabin, partly because of the high composition of premium fare traffic in general and first class in particular. Consider the following statistic. It is estimated that across the Atlantic, 10 percent of the passengers paying premium fares generate 40 percent of the revenue. In the JFK-Heathrow market, about 5 percent of the passengers generate 30 percent of the revenue.

There is no general answer to the question of fragmentation versus consolidation. Unfortunately, up to this point, sufficient market research has not been conducted to provide definitive answers to the question of the cost benefits of separate airplanes for separate traffic segments. As pointed out in Chapter 1, passengers say one thing in surveys and do another in their actual purchase behavior. The only reasonable way to get such answers is to experiment just as Lufthansa is doing. Consequently, a reasonable option for large airlines is to try things out, exemplified by the operations of Lufthansa—limited routes flown by dedicated corporate aircraft.

While the use of single aisle aircraft in all business class configurations appears to be doing well, the applications for this business model appear to be limited. When looking at purely trans-Atlantic premium fare passengers (paying, for example, $1,500 or more for one way fare), there are only a couple of dozen markets that have 30 or more premium passengers per day each way. Conversely, there are well over 100 markets that have between 5 and 30 passengers per day each way. Similar to the success of regional jets in North America and Europe for service in relatively long and thin markets, there is a significant potential opportunity for an airline to exploit some thin trans-Atlantic markets with a regional jet like product. Such a product could differentiate itself from the "single factory" wide body aircraft in the following way:

- A small aircraft can offer high touch, personalized passenger service from the cabin and flight crew.

- Time is the ultimate luxury for some travelers, a luxury that is often absent in today's commercial travel. A small aircraft takes very little time to load and unload, especially compared to a wide body aircraft. This feature reduces the time required for passengers to show up prior to the departure time.

- Providing direct service where none existed previously is another time saver for some passengers. Moreover, direct service reduces the risk of missed connections for one stop service.

- Frequency has value for some premium fare passengers and, as with the regional jets, can be less expensive to add to existing routes with smaller aircraft.

There is a class of ultra long haul (ULH) corporate aircraft (for example, those produced by manufacturers such as Bombardier and Gulfstream) that could be reconfigured for this application. At first glance, the perceived risks of the use of ULH corporate aircraft to test thin premium passenger markets appear to be high. However, the risk and cost of using ULH corporate aircraft is not necessarily prohibitive when compared to using alternative aircraft to test the concept. An ULH corporate aircraft may not be cost effective in the long run to operate dedicated service, as compared to similar sized commercial aircraft that are designed for the mission profile, namely, 6-10 hour flights and 5000+ block hours per year utilization with a high degree of reliability. However, it can play an important role in testing the concept of a point-to-point trans-Atlantic service for premium passengers—either or Business class in markets thinner than those viable for the 40 seat single aisle commercial airliners. Assuming that the concept works with a ULH corporate aircraft, a commercial aircraft manufacturer could supply an aircraft to meet an airline's operational requirements. There are sufficient markets for such type of operations, as previously discussed, that a manufacturer could be interested if the production were to be in the range of 50-100 units. Again, while the costs of using the ULH business jet would be high, that is only to test the market and refine the business concept with relatively low risk. To start the experiment, the proof-of-concept aircraft can be refurbished with either 10-15 or 20-25 business class seats. Figure 4.1 shows an example of the layout of a business class cabin in a Bombardier's Global Express.

Another line of thinking is to use an existing single aisle aircraft with, say, 10 first class seats or 20 business class seats and fill the remaining section of the fuselage with economy seats as much as possible. At first glance this concept seams more cost effective than the previously discussed ULH dedicated corporate aircraft. However, the ULH corporate aircraft will have lower cash operating costs. Furthermore, even the higher ownership cost is not straight forward.

First, there is the issue of how to compute certain ownership cost. Does one assume that the single aisle aircraft is fully depreciated and therefore the cost is zero or does one assume that if such an aircraft is taken out of revenue service, it would need to be replaced with another, possibly new, aircraft? If a new aircraft had to be purchased to backfill, then there would be an opportunity cost.

**Figure 4.1   An Example of the Cabin Layout in an Ultra Long
             Haul Corporate Aircraft**
Source: Bombardier Aerospace.

The next consideration relates to the reliability of the used single aisle aircraft vs. a new aircraft. This raises the question of how many spare aircraft might be needed to meet or exceed the schedule completion targets. Next, there is the issue of what if the concept does not work? Then the airline would need to absorb the cost of refurbishing the old aircraft, particularly the cost of modifications for the extra fuel tanks. An ULH corporate aircraft would not require costly modifications such as the extra fuel tanks and with a new interior could be sold back into the corporate aircraft market in its reconfigured form.

There are equally important questions on the revenue side of the equation. There are the revenue cannibalization issues to consider. A single aisle aircraft configured with 40 seats would have a lower average fare than a 20 seat ULH corporate aircraft. Would the dilution in fare make the operation unprofitable? What would happen if the 40 business class passengers are cannibalized from existing scheduled aircraft service? Would that now make existing services on the large airplane unprofitable? Would the existing larger aircraft now have to been down gauged to a smaller sized aircraft?

The best aircraft is the one that satisfies passenger market demand with the lowest trip costs and with seat costs well below the average fare and, therefore, maximizes profitability. The idea is to consider only the point-to-point passenger demand, no connecting passengers. The final selection would depend on passenger demand for the particular route that the airline is going to serve. The corporate aircraft is much more cost effective on a trip cost basis for the thinner markets such as 10 O&D passenger per day each way. Moreover, in the fare consideration, the airline cannot overlook the potential for market stimulation due to the availability of nonstop service and passengers' willingness to pay more for direct service. On the other side of the coin, having economy class seats that are "virtually free" degrades the value of the first class product due to the added complexity of handling 100 additional passengers in the economy class.

On the other side, the case for consolidation is clear. Most long haul intercontinental markets call for big airplanes and a multi-class service and high frequency. Large airplanes provide the economies of aircraft density—that is low unit operating costs. The consolidation process also helps an airline leverage the interrelationship between products and network (particularly the breadth of the network). Product and network strategies are interconnected. There are also alliance considerations, whether they relate to other mainline code sharing partners, regional affiliates, franchisees, or subsidiaries. The negative side of consolidation is that not only are there problems from the view point of premium paying customers (who do not want to mix with passengers buying lower levels of service), but airlines find it difficult to deal with separately branded products on the same aircraft. Consolidation leads to managing customer expectations. Using separate airplanes for different segments will reduce this problem.

Based on the concerns expressed by many customers, there is clearly a need for a product that falls between the economy class and business class in intercontinental markets. Virgin was the very first one to develop such a product (premium economy) for passengers paying the top end of the economy fare. This product is also proving to be very popular with high end leisure travelers and business travelers when they are paying out of their own pockets. This product is also very good during recessions when business people do not want to pay the full business class fares. Figure 4.2 shows a typical premium economy seat configuration (38 inch pitch).

Figure 4.2 Virgin Atlantic's Premium Economy Class Seats
Source: Virgin Atlantic Airways.

When Condor was a charter subsidiary of Lufthansa in the 1990s, it developed a very basic business class section in its 767s flying across the Atlantic. It was highly successful because the difference in price was very reasonable, 800 DM at the back and 1600 DM at the front. The seat pitch was only 40 inches. That particular example is an excellent case study because it was done on a design-to-cost basis, something that Toyota does with its cars. The basic concept is really simple: Find out what the customer will pay for a product and then design the product for that price.

There is clearly a need for more "Business Lite" products similar to the premium economy products developed originally by Virgin

Atlantic. Consider the information contained in Figures 4.3 and 4.4. A mere 10 percent of the passengers generate 40 percent of the revenue. Would not a modified business class product in the region of $2,500 round trip be successful? The caveat would be the difficulty in comparing costs: the analyses become complicated as costs and revenues are drilled down in detail.

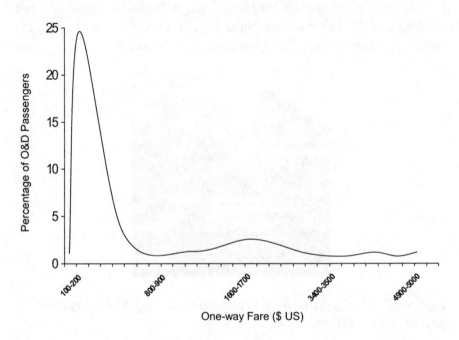

Figure 4.3 An Estimate of the Fare Distribution in Trans-Atlantic Markets

The renovation can be in the aircraft, on the ground, or in the pricing system. As stated earlier, fare structures currently work backwards. It started with a very high "normal economy" fare and came down with each restriction. Would it not make more sense to have a very low basic fare and then allow the customer to purchase product features in incremental value (value added pricing vs. discount based pricing). Such a product and fare structure not only un-bundles the previous product features but also re-bundles existing and new features (both physical and intangible) into new offerings

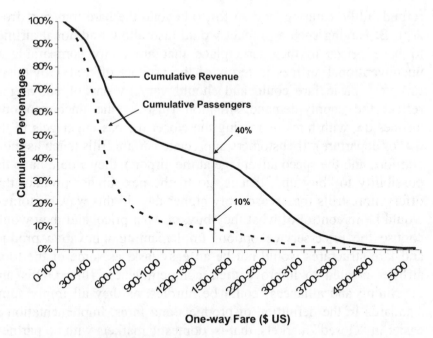

**Figure 4.4   An Estimate of Passenger and Revenue Distribution
in Trans-Atlantic Markets**

targeted at different customer segments, with different needs and different willingness to pay for such products.[4] Figure 4.5 shows an example developed by McKinsey on what such a fare scheme might look like in short haul markets. The added benefit of such a system is that besides being customer-oriented it also creates an opportunity in which some customers may "buy-up", just because they see that for, say, 20-30 dollars more they can get a better product, that is, a product whose features (for example, refundability, or better comfort) they value in excess of the additional price.[5] The information shown is for illustrative purposes only.

Using such a product-fare architecture, customers would start from the "bottom", where they get the "no frills" product. In order to access this fare, customers would need to do everything by themselves (booking online, using self-service check-in and so forth), would have to come early to the airport, and they would not get any of the additional benefits (miles, assigned seats, flexibility, refundability, catering, and so forth) beyond the bare transport from A to B. Having such a product would also allow traditional airlines to have prices in the marketplace that are really comparable to unconventional airlines in terms of the product offered. Obviously, this very basic fare could and should vary by day of booking to reflect the supply-demand situation (just as the unconventional airlines do, with fares increasing the closer the passenger gets to the day of departure). If customers appreciate certain frills (such as more comfort, and the speed advantage at the airport), they would have the possibility to "buy up", that is, go to the next higher product that offers more frills for a reasonably higher fare. In this way, customers would be in control of what they buy, at what price, and they would choose the price-service option. Implementing innovative product and fare structures would not be an easy task, as some of the tools airlines created to improve their competitiveness (like GDSs and interlining and alliances) could be hurdles, as they all imply some standards in the definition of products and fares. Implementation is easier in "closed" markets, that is, domestic markets with no partners to interline with, and with a very high share of online distribution. GDSs can also be used for developing innovative products as long as the new fare products follow the standard logic. As shown in Chapter 2, Air Canada has recently moved to a similar approach, offering just five branded fare types and removing many of the old style restrictions.

Monitoring Game Changing Competitors

Recent Successes

Despite the lower quality of service offered by some unconventional carriers (for example, high density one class seating), these airlines still offer value for money. Moreover, some unconventional airlines earn a lot of revenue from ancillary sources. Ryanair, for example, is earning a significant proportion of its revenue from ancillary sources, selling car rentals, food, hotel rooms, and so forth. In fact, one wonders if they make any money on selling air travel? All the profit

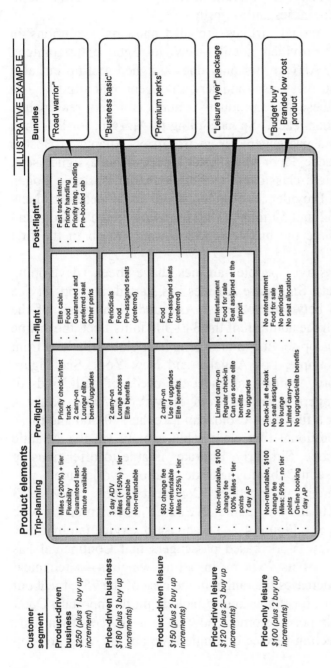

Figure 4.5 Bundling Simple Products to Needs of Different Customer Segments
Source: Pompeo, Lucio (McKinsey & Company), "Paradigm Shift— Changing Rules for Airlines", A presentation made at the IATA Finance Committee, New York, April 2005, p. 15.

is coming from either high margin ancillary revenue or subsidies from airports, communities and so forth.

Other unconventional airlines are also showing evolutions in products. jetBlue provided totally new in-flight entertainment, including live TV. AirTran not only does assigned seating but also has a reasonable business class and serves conventional airports. The price for each of these three products features is a very reasonable, about 25 to 30 dollars each. So, according to AirTran, for less than 100 dollars more, a passenger can go from say, Atlanta to Boston (instead of Providence, RI or Manchester, NH) with an assigned seat, a seat in the business class cabin and an arrival at Boston's Logan International, not Providence, Rhode Island or Manchester, New Hampshire, each 52 and 59 miles away from downtown Boston, and the destination where the business person wants to go in the first place.

For time sensitive people airlines have been developing appropriate products. Singapore Airlines has started nonstop service across the Pacific between Southeast Asia and both coasts of the United States. With the addition of the 340-500 in its fleet, the airline is able to offer nonstop service in ultra long haul global markets from Singapore—for example, Los Angeles and New York. See Figure 4.6. Now Singapore Airlines can meet the needs of both kinds of passengers. Passengers boarding from New York, who prefer a nonstop flight over a first class cabin, can take the 340-500 and those who prefer the traditional first class cabin can fly via the Atlantic with a stop in Europe. Similarly, Emirates is able to offer nonstop service from its base in Dubai to major destinations worldwide.

From a different perspective, Continental now serves 13 transatlantic markets and one market in South America nonstop with a single aisle 757. See Figure 4.7. The nonstop service is obviously so popular with New York based passengers that Continental has extended the range of its 757s by installing winglets—a technical modification that increases the range, in the case of the 757, by about 200 miles, sufficient for the airline to include more important O&D markets within Europe. Customers now have a choice—twin aisle aircraft with connecting service or single aisle aircraft with nonstop service.

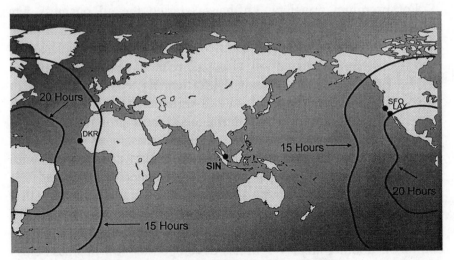

Figure 4.6 Nonstop Service Singapore-New York
Source: Based on Paul Clark (AirBusiness Academy), Presentation
made at The Ohio State University and Continental Airlines
12th International Airline Symposium, January 17-19, 2005,
Honolulu, Hawaii, USA.

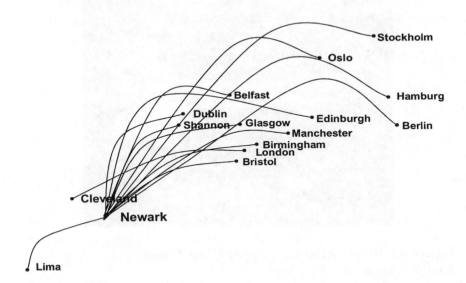

Figure 4.7 Continental's Nonstop Service with 757s

For premium travelers, Lufthansa started the all business jets across the Atlantic in three markets. Air France introduced a quite different product (a two class cabin with a small business class) for passengers from Paris to oil and gas related destinations in the Middle East, Africa, and Russia. Unfortunately, customers living in very small towns still need to use hub-and-spoke systems. For such passengers, Lufthansa recently introduced a new product developed jointly with NetJets to transport premium passengers from 1,000 airports within Europe to Munich to make connections with Lufthansa's flights. So, a passenger from Lugano, Switzerland can now fly in a NetJets corporate aircraft to Munich and connect with a Lufthansa flight to Los Angeles. Network is not the only area where game changing competitors are introducing new products. Creature comfort is another area. Virgin has developed its new business class (Upper Class Suites) that is reported to be as good as if not better than most first class cabins but priced at business class fares, shown in Figure 4.8.

Figure 4.8 Virgin Atlantic's Upper Class Cabin
Source: Virgin Atlantic Airways

For its premium class passengers traveling in intercontinental markets, Lufthansa developed a completely separate terminal at

Frankfurt. The idea is that Lufthansa can take advantage of the economies of scale and use the same aircraft to transport everyone but introduce differentiation by keeping the premium passengers away from the masses, taking care of all their needs at this dedicated terminal, including security (no hassles) and being whisked to the aircraft in Porsche SUVs or a Mercedes S-class. The reason for using Porsche is presumably to give the image of speed. Passengers do not leave the terminal until the pilot is almost ready to push back. See Figure 4.9.

Figure 4.9   Lufthansa's Dedicated Terminal and Transfer to Aircraft at Frankfurt Airport for First Class Passengers

Source: Lufthansa German Airlines.

New Efforts

There are a number of areas where airlines have taken initiatives to move further along the renovation continuum. Here are two examples. A number of airlines worldwide have introduced nonstop service with regional jets in markets where trip time is approaching almost four hours. Table 4.1 shows the 11 longest haul city pairs for regional jets in the world. Here the jury is still out. Some passengers will not fly in regional jets for more than two hours. Others are clearly taking trips approaching four hours. Apparently, passengers will make such long trips if the service is nonstop and the cabin configuration is reasonably comfortable.

Some airlines have found it cost effective to deploy jet-like speed, quiet and comfort, with the favorable economics of turboprop aircraft in the regional jet sector markets. FlyBe (based in the UK) is using the Q400 (a 70 seat turboprop) to implement an offensive strategy, aimed at (a) competing directly with easyJet in thinner markets, (b) gaining market share from British Airways, and (c) offering low fare service in regional markets. In contrast, Horizon Air (based in the US) has used the same aircraft to implement a defensive strategy, aimed at (a) maintaining market share in competing with Southwest, (b) providing high frequency service in regional markets, and (c) obtaining a fare premium over Southwest in some markets. As an example of the last point, in some markets, Horizon Air has been able to achieve a greater passenger market share compared to frequency share in competition with Southwest, while charging a higher fare.[6]

Airlines are also experimenting with three class service in key US transcontinental markets. United, for example, is testing its premium service on some flights between New York and Los Angeles and between New York and San Francisco. The airline took 70 seats out of a 757 and converted the remaining 120 seats into three classes—first, business and economy-plus (which has slightly higher seat pitch than standard seat in the economy class). The first class section has lie-flat beds similar to those used in intercontinental markets.[7] Are there other options worth exploring? Could luxurious under floor lounges be cost effective—with basic seats for takeoff and landing and the space to be adapted to provide workspace or crew rest areas?

Figure 4.10 shows clearly the ramification of product-price strategies of conventional airlines, focused primarily on revenue with costs being "controlled" in a random manner. Unconventional airlines, on the other hand, established patterns that primarily control

Table 4.1 The Longest Markets Served by Regional Jets

City Pair	Distance Miles	Trip Time Minutes	Airline
Austin, Texas-San Francisco, California	1,493	235	United
Boise, Idaho-Houston, Texas	1,482	220	Continental
Los Angeles, California-Morelia, Mexico	1,443	205	Continental
Kiev, Ukraine-Tehran, Iran	1,437	150	Saro
Bakersfield, California-Houston, Texas	1,425	216	Continental
Frankfurt, Germany-Rostov, Russia	1,422	215	Lufthansa
Chicago, Illinois-Edmonton, Alberta	1, 418	225	United
Phoenix, Arizona-Edmonton, Alberta	1,376	205	America West
Los Angeles, California-Fayetteville, Arkansas	1,368	182	American
Los Angeles, California-Edmonton, Alberta	1,360	204	America West
Larnaca, Cyprus-Warsaw, Poland	1,349	210	LOT Polish

Source: March 2005 World Airline Schedules.

costs by remaining focused on their product-price model. This focus has enabled them to remain profitable when revenues fell—often because of their market presence.

It is interesting to note that in recent years a number of unconventional airlines diverted from their original low-cost leadership strategy (based on Southwest) to implement a product differentiation strategy. In the US, for example, the product offered by Southwest is quite different from Frontier. Similarly, in Europe, the product offered by Ryanair is quite different from Virgin Express. The differences exist not only in areas related to the marketing aspects of products (for example, services and distribution) but also to operations (for example, network and fleet). One recent analysis shows that even with limited differentiation in the product offered the unconventional airlines have been able to achieve profitability. However, there is some evidence that those unconventional airlines that adhered more closely to the original low-cost business model (such as Ryanair and easyJet) have achieved higher operating profit margins.[8]

While the Revenue per Available Seat Mile (RASM) of unconventional airlines remains lower than that of conventional airlines, their RASM has always remained higher than their Cost per Available Seat Mile (CASM). The inability of the legacy model to maintain the RASM above the CASM, not once, but for two extended periods in the past 15 years, proves that while it is very easy to be a low fare airline, it is much more difficult to be low fare and low cost. The consequences of that imbalance may be fatal.

Seeking and Creating Innovation

Beyond product renovation airlines must think about product innovation to meet the dramatically changing needs of consumers and emerging technology. The following are some examples:

- If the leisure-VFR segment of the marketplace is the one growing at the fastest rate, and if the three most important criteria for this segment are price, price and price, and if the

380 promises to provide the lowest unit operating costs, then why not consider operating a 380 in high density configuration (750 seats) in high density markets (for example, New York to London and Los Angeles to London)? To meet the simplicity needs of the leisure-VFR segment, the service could have just two prices—US$100 each way from New York and $150 from Los Angeles, every seat, every day. Tickets could be non-refundable but usable for future flights on a standby basis. Ancillary revenue could be generated on board for simple activities such as limited menus containing pre-packaged cold food and beverages and rental systems for in-flight entertainment. The operation needs to resemble a train service. For example, train service employees do not have systems for handling passengers' bags. Passengers are responsible for handling their own bags. Porter service could be made available. Undoubtedly, a lot of analyses need to be conducted to determine the economic viability. Would there be insufficient demand for such a large airplane even in high density markets, especially during the off-peak periods? What if the flights served Stansted Airport so that passengers could take advantage of low fare continuing flights? There would be no interlining, it could act similar to the operations of Icelandair, where they had informal connections from their Luxembourg hub with buses and trains. How much stimulation in demand could be forecast? How could routes be selected to provide maximum utilization of aircraft?

- Commercial airline service in short haul thin markets in the US has become unattractive for customers, given the traditional airlines' economic need to go through hub-and-spoke systems coupled with the additional time required for security processing. The demand for 50 seat aircraft has plateaued (some say disappeared) and regional jet manufacturers are moving toward larger 70-100 seat aircraft. Thus, there may be an unfulfilled demand for a point-to-point domestic service. Technology is now available to use four-seat very lights jets (VLJ) in an air taxi service. Again, the feasibility of this concept needs to be examined in light of the projected demand, the operating costs of VLJs, the operational capabilities of thousands of small airports and the information technology to establish an efficient dispatch system. For example, a passenger could call for a 4 PM departure. There could be another call from the same catchment area for a departure at 4:30 PM. Consumer engagement is needed to determine if either passenger would be willing to change the departure time to save money. Some entrepreneurs are convinced that the concept is viable to the point that they have announced their plans to begin services by the middle of 2006.[9]

- What is the economic feasibility of prepaid airline fare cards? For example, for travel within US domestic markets, could a large conventional airline offer for $30,000 a guaranteed seat in first class on any flight and without a reservation? The passenger simply shows up at an airport and it is the responsibility of the airline to accommodate that passenger. The same service could be offered for $20,000 for travel in economy class, or even for $5,000 on a standby basis. Airlines obviously have access to sophisticated revenue management systems to determine the viability of such products. As for handling standby passengers, again airlines have systems already in place to accommodate travel by airline employees and their families.

- A major problem experienced by most travelers, at least within the US, is the extra time needed for processing as a result of additional security related requirements. Additional time is only one part of the problem. Uncertainty as to how much time should be allowed is another component of the problem. Why not really go out of the way and develop new ways of airport processing by working closely with airports and governments. Airlines, airports, and government officials all point to the difficulties involved in coordinating the activities of the three organizations. Surely, this must be a high priority area where the product could be improved significantly for the mutual benefit of all. Could the immigration-customs pre-clearance process in place in such countries as Canada and Ireland be expanded to other countries?

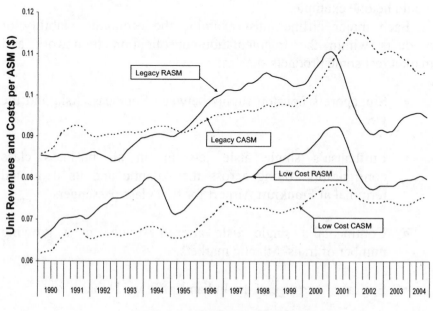

Figure 4.10 The Importance of Balance between RASM and CASM

Source: US Department of Transportation Data Banks.

Conclusions

Airlines must renovate and, in some cases, innovate their product portfolio to adapt to the changes in the marketplace. These changes include (a) the change in the traffic mix, customer concerns and expectations within the traffic mix and different growth rates within the traffic mix, (b) the entry of a broad spectrum of new competitors (discussed in Chapter 2), and (c) the availability of aircraft technology from the ultra long haul airplanes for intercontinental markets to regional jets for long haul domestic and regional markets to cost effective turboprops. Products that provide neither value for the customer nor profit for the airline need to be eliminated. A certain segment of the traffic moving over hub-and-spoke systems would be one example.

Each major airline must examine the economic viability of products within the fragmentation-consolidation framework and market test some products such as:

- Singapore's nonstop flights between Southeast Asia and the US.

- Lufthansa's single aisle jets in an all business class configuration flying across the Atlantic and its dedicated terminal at Frankfurt Airport for first class passengers.

- Continental's single aisle aircraft service in a growing number of trans-Atlantic markets.

- Emirates' carriage of the Indian traffic via Dubai.

- FlyBe's low fare services in regional markets with turboprop aircraft.

Given the increase in price consciousness for all categories of passengers, there is a clear need for value based products such as the premium economy class services offered by Virgin Atlantic and British Airways. Airlines also need to examine their product-price policies from another perspective. The conventional airlines' current structure is penalty based and needs to be unbundled and re-bundled to promote "buy-up". In the final analyses:

- Conventional airlines must learn lessons from unconventional airlines to find a favorable balance between RASM and

CASM, a balance that can be sustained over a long period of time.

- All airlines can learn from Toyota's design-to-cost framework, namely, find out what the customer will pay for a product and then design the product for that price.

- Airlines must focus—as they are beginning to do in Europe— on the ground product, getting passengers through the airport faster.

Notes

[1] On the other hand, a greater number of passengers would enable an airline to use a larger aircraft that, in turn, would have lower unit operating costs.

[2] Shaw, Stephen, *Airline Marketing and Management*, 5th Ed. (Aldershot, UK: Ashgate, 2004). p. 143.

[3] Hedley, Barry D., "Strategy and the 'Business Portfolio'", *Long Range Planning*, Volume 10, Number 1, February 1977, pp. 9-15.

[4] Pompeo, Lucio (McKinsey & Company), "Paradigm Shift—Changing Rules for Airlines", A presentation made at the IATA Finance Committee, New York, April 6, 2005, p. 13.

[5] Pompeo, Lucio (McKinsey & Company), "Paradigm Shift—Changing Rules for Airlines", A presentation made at the IATA Finance Committee, New York, April 6, 2005, p. 14.

[6] Three markets were analyzed: Boise-Spokane (287 statute miles), Boise-Seattle (399 statute miles), and Portland-Spokane (279 statute miles) for the period 2nd Quarter 2004 using the data from airline guides and the US Department of Transportation—O&D and Onboard.

[7] Maynard, Micheline, "Budget Airlines Set Off on a Cross-Country Joy Ride", *The New York Times*, 03 April, 2005, ytimes.com, p. 2.

[8] Alamdari, Fariba, "Impact of the Adherence to the Original Low-cost Model on the Profitability of Low-cost Airlines", *Transport Review*, Volume 25, Number 3, May 2005, pp. 377-392.

[9] Lunsford, Lynn, "Air-Taxi Venture Set to Start Service in Mid-2006", *Wall Street Journal*, April 25, 2005, p. B4.

Chapter 5

Pricing for Mutual Benefit

Despite liberalization of the global airline industry to varying degrees in various parts of the world, with the exception of Southwest's operations in the US, passengers have had limited price-service options until the beginning of this century. As such, they continued to accept, although grudgingly, the value proposition of conventional airlines. In the past five or six years, however, the phenomenonal expansion of unconventional airlines and technology have provided customers with genuine price-service options. Passengers are empowered to select their desired price-service combinations. Business travelers, in particular, are able to *see* the premiums they pay. Transparent fares and services displayed on the Internet have allowed consumers a new degree of choice enabled by side-by-side comparisons, and alternate airports or dates where even better bargains can be found.

Chapter 2 treated the hypercompetitive environment, where major airlines have already lost a significant amount of pricing power as a result of the:

- Unconventional airlines achieving a critical mass in North America and in Europe.

- The increasing acceptance of the products offered by unconventional airlines.

- The commoditization of the airline product in short and medium haul developed markets.

- The yield realities of the US domestic and intra-European markets expanding to key intercontinental markets.

This chapter explores the implications of these trends on airline pricing policies and examines the balance between passengers' desires for value, choice and simplicity and any airline's need for sustainable long term profitability.

Reviewing Passenger Concerns with Pricing Strategies

Perceived Unfairness

Consumer behavior has changed as a result of numerous factors, the most important being the expansion of services offered by unconventional airlines (discussed in Chapter 2) and the expansion of information technology. Travelers quickly accepted the deployment of fare search and booking engines. They are willing to buy online, and they are finding the products offered by the unconventional airlines to be not only acceptable but in some cases more desirable. This change in consumer behavior alone has forced the legacy major network airlines to implement major changes in their fare structure and fare levels. In this new environment, passengers actively shun anything that resembles the old fare structure, which they always viewed to be unfair, irrational, suspicious and bewildering.

Business passengers found the fare structure to be unfair because it forced them to purchase full fare tickets at prices up to ten times the level of discounted tickets. Fares are still very high in markets where there is no effective competition with the unconventional airlines.

Passengers did not like the fare structure because they did not understand why fares differed so much. Airlines knew that fares contained bundled features but the passengers did not know that. In the case of the leisure traveler, prices for point-to-point service in a local domestic market may have contained the cost of interlining with international airlines. In the case of corporate travel, when the airline sold a ticket to a corporate traveler, the price included a commission paid to the agent. The agent then rebated part of the ticket price back to the corporation. In the process the agent built some product features that added value for some corporations but not others—a fare auditing capability, a quality control capability, and reports containing various kinds of information. These product features became standard and few questioned their viability from the point of view of who paid for them. Ultimately, the customer paid for these product features. There was no accountability regarding the cost and the benefits of such features.

Business passengers resent, not so much the concept of having to pay a premium fare for having flexibility and for avoiding restrictions, but the amount of premium paid. Flexibility costs more than five times the lowest fare. Should such a difference be no more than a factor of two or three at the most? There is no realistic market research that sheds any light in this area. While leisure passengers can comprehend advance purchase, they have difficulty in the logic of the Saturday night stay and why a one-way ticket often costs more than a round-trip ticket. While passengers can see the reason for a fee to change a reservation, they cannot see the reasoning of $100 on a ticket that cost $175 in the first place.

Passengers feel that fare structures are irrational because they bear no relationship to distance. In some cases, passengers traveling in the Chicago-New York, or Cincinnati-New York, or Cleveland-New York local markets and those traveling between the same three US cities and London, England pay the same fare. Even after the airlines have put a limit on the full economy fares, there is still irrationality from a passenger's perspective. Consider the full economy fare between Pittsburgh and Dayton, Ohio ($956), between Pittsburgh and Denver, Colorado ($998), and Pittsburgh and San Francisco, California ($1,018). The fares are almost identical and yet the differences in the distances traveled is almost 2000 miles.[1] Passengers point to another irrationality in the fare structure. Why do passengers traveling on a nonstop flight pay the same fare as others flying with connecting service?

A Lack of Integrity

Passengers also have an integrity problem with airline fares. No passenger can be sure if a particular fare will be available in the next two hours, days, weeks, or months. How can passengers plan their businesses when their travel costs change so much? Can a person calculate how much six trips to a destination will cost in the next three months? Can a business person say to a potential client, "OK, I will be there tomorrow", knowing roughly what it will cost, or be distracted from going because of the uncertainty regarding the fare— will it be $100 or $1,000? How can any business plan on exploring opportunities in a new city if they do not know what the travel costs will be?

Passengers suspect that airlines will try to get away with whatever they can. Passengers are so used to being taken advantage of, that their defenses are up any time a conventional airline introduces something new. On the US domestic front, airlines claim that by removing truly restrictive conditions such as advance purchase and Saturday night stay, there is now less distinction in fares between leisure travel and business travel. The perception and the reality remain that fares are simply a question of what the competition is doing and what an airline can get away with. Consider the market between Philadelphia and Pittsburgh—a distance of about 300 miles. At the beginning of March 2005, the unrestricted fare was US$335 one way (excluding various government taxes, airport charges and security charges). This fare represents a yield of one dollar and 12 cents, more than 9 times the 12 cents average yield per mile in the US markets.

On top of all of the aforementioned concerns, one hears about how bewildering airline fares are. The real concern is about fares being (a) reasonable and (b) being available on an everyday basis. People are concerned about the degree of complexity. Consumers value and want ease of doing business. Some people have more time and some people have more money. Some are willing to pay for convenience and some are not. Some will pay more for the ability to make a booking at the last minute; others will not. Customers want choice and making choices available leads to a certain level of complexity. However, complexity must be comprehensible and not bewildering.

To put some of these comments in perspective, it may be helpful to examine the fare structure and levels in a given market, say between New York (JFK) and London (LHR). Table 5.1 shows the published fare structure during the first week of March 2005 for various classes of service. All fares quoted represent the average of two brand airlines. Fares shown do not include taxes that range from US$148 to US$190. Some published fares are discounted.

Table 5.1 Fare Structure, New York-London, March 2005 (US$)

Class of Service	Return Fare
First Class	$12,690
Business class	$ 8,365
Premium Economy	$ 2,010
Normal Economy	$ 1,330
Discounted Economy	$ 270

Source: Airlines' Websites.

One can see there is an enormous variation in the fares, ranging from $270 to $12,690. Depending on the class of service and fare restrictions, the variation in fares (first, business and premium economy) reflect cost considerations for products offered on the ground (separate check-in lines, access to airport lounges) and in the airplane (seat pitch and width, additional flight attendants, in-flight meals and entertainment). They also include the cost of less visible features such as the presence or absence of restrictions.

Price Ratio not Justified by Product Features

Passengers have another major issue in pricing, especially for international code-shared flights: Seats on the same airplane (operated by one partner) can be sold for wildly different amounts by different partners. In trans-Pacific markets customers have seen fares range from $3,000 to $6,000 for business class, depending on the partner selling the ticket. Similarly, economy class tickets can be obtained for anywhere between $1,100 and $1,600 for travel on the same airplane, again, depending on the partner with which the passenger chooses to make the booking.

While customers recognize the fare differential among different cabins, they do not perceive any difference in the fares types in the economy class. These fares vary from $1,330 to $270. The heavily discounted fare of $270 has the most restrictions. There are seven other fares (between $270 and $1,330) apparently to meet different needs of different segments, but in reality to comply with the fences. The top end fare ($1,330) is completely flexible with respect to changes, is refundable and has much greater availability up to the point of departure.

Let us begin with an analysis of the price differential between normal economy and premium economy. If one were to assume the cost of flexibility to be $1,060 (the difference between $1,330 and $270), one could assume that the cost of additional product features (such as extra space, 38 inch pitch vs. 31 inch seat pitch and a separate cabin) is $680 (the difference between $2,010 and $1,330). These differences in fares and product features appear to have some logic. However, consumers are confused by fare breakdowns within economy class. Consumers understand refundable vs. non-refundable, but they do not understand why the $200 fare that was available yesterday is now $325? It is still nonrefundable and appears to have no additional benefit. They understand that the previous fare is "sold out" but what does that mean? And why don't they know how many seats are left at that price?

As to the difference in fares between cabins, many passengers have difficulty in understanding the difference between $2,010 for premium economy class and $8,365 for business class. If the cost of flexibility is $1,060 within the economy class (according to the preceding estimate), the cost of flexibility is now up to $6,355 ($8,365-$2,010) between premium economy and business class! It is difficult for passengers to accept that this difference can be accounted for by such product features as a bigger seat and better meals. Finally, there is the difference between first class fares ($12,690) and business class fares ($8,365), reflecting even more subtle differences in product features and exclusivity.[2]

This table illustrates passenger concerns for the complexity of the fare structure, the high cost of flexibility by cabin, the restrictions (some of which do not make any sense to the passenger—such as the requirement for Saturday night stay), and the exceptionally high cost of certain product features. Consumers also do not understand why "hidden city" and the so called "nested tickets" are so frowned upon by airlines. Passengers ask that if a passenger finds a loophole, why they shouldn't be allowed to take advantage of it?

Passengers' concerns are not with the overall logic but the degree to which the logic has been applied. Corporate travel managers are becoming increasingly outraged at the international fares in premium cabins. It is interesting to note the lengths they have gone to cut costs. In one case, management was considering sending the passenger in business class on the outbound leg so that the passenger could be relaxed and productive for the meeting and bringing the passenger back in economy class.

Sensing Pricing-Related Emerging Forces

Real Yield Declining

Passenger yield has been declining (in real terms) since the beginning of the air transportation industry. See Figure 5.1. Until recently, these declines were accompanied by similar declines in costs from the increased productivity of aircraft, labor and systems. While the continuing decline in yield is not news, what is news is that the:

- high-paying passengers are disappearing, or

- they are now flying in the back due to a change in corporate polices, or

- they are buying more back-to-back tickets, or

- booking on cheap fares and if the travel plans change, simply throwing away the cheap ticket, or

- using a bid system such as with Priceline (for private travel).

The availability of price-service options by the unconventional airlines has had an enormous impact on the revenue side of the equation without a comparable impact on the cost side.

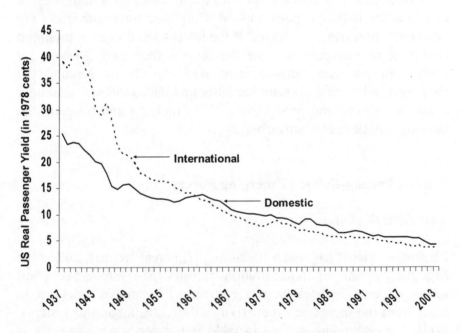

Figure 5.1 The Continuing Decline in Passenger Yield
Source: Air Transport Association of America.

Figure 5.2 shows the impact on the conventional airlines' segmented business model—high fares for travelers with little or no flexibility and a broad spectrum of low fares for travelers with flexibility. Although it may not appear to be reasonable from some passengers' perspective, this pricing practice is consistent with economic theory.[3] The vertical line marked SIFL (standard industry fare level) represents a hypothetical number that if everyone on an airplane paid this standard fare, the airline would generate a reasonable return on investment. Data on either side of the SIFL line shows the percentage of revenue generated by passengers paying different amounts above and below the SIFL number. Clearly, there were a small number of passengers paying very high fares and a very large number of passengers paying a very low fare. This situation has been deteriorating since the late 1990s, moving more and more passengers from the right (high fares) to the left (low fares). Even with an improving economy, a high percentage of the passengers who took advantage of lower fares will not return to purchase higher priced tickets.

High Fare Traffic Volume Shrinking

The major problem from the airlines' perspective can be demonstrated by the data shown in Figure 5.3. The number of passengers traveling on high fares is decreasing. Consider the distribution of O&D passengers by fare type in the market between Los Angeles' International Airport and New York' LaGuardia Airport between the third quarter of 2000 and the third quarter of 2004. The number of passengers traveling at high fares (more than $500 each way) decreased from 10 percent to 4 percent while the number of passengers traveling at low fares (between $100 and $200) increased from 36 percent to 60 percent. Moreover, while the total number of passengers is down by 28 percent in this four year period, the total revenue is down by 45 percent (from a combination of 28 percent reduction in passengers and a 24 percent reduction in fares). This example illustrates the changing situation even more dramatically when one considers the fact that there is no low fare airline flying nonstop in this market. The dilution in revenue is due primarily to the introduction of a low fare service by jetBlue between New York's JFK Airport and Los Angeles' Long Beach Airport and a number of other airlines that serve this market with connections through their base of operations.

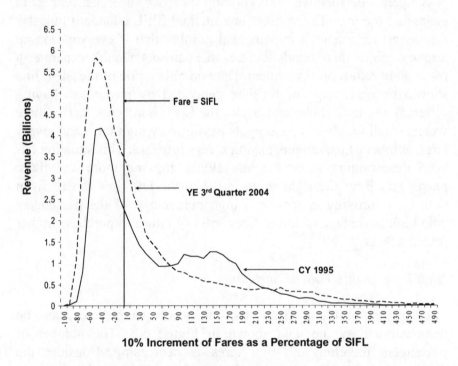

Figure 5.2 Distribution of Industry Origin-Destination Revenue: US Contiguous 48 State Markets
Source: US Department of Transportation Data Banks.

The decrease in the number of passengers traveling at higher fares on conventional airlines can be accounted for by another aspect of the value proposition introduced by some unconventional airlines. Consider, for example, the ticket nonrefundability rules of easyJet. A business passenger could buy an advance purchase, nonrefundable ticket at a low fare. If the passenger's plans change, the nonrefundable ticket can be changed by paying a penalty of £10 per leg plus the difference in fares between the two flights (the new flight desired and the old flight booked).[4]

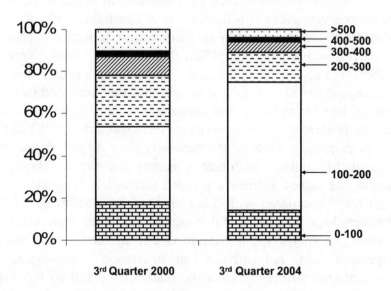

Los Angeles-New York (LaGuardia Airport)
Passenger Distribution by Fare Type

**Figure 5.3 Distribution of Passengers by Fare Type in the Los
Angeles-New York (LaGuardia) Market, 3rd Quarter
2000 and 2004**
Source: US Department of Transportation Data Banks.

A recent survey conducted in the UK of 264 business travelers
suggested that when making short haul trips, they only change their
tickets in 31 percent of trips.[5] Consequently, according to some
research, even with fees for changes and the difference in the fare
between last minute and advance purchase travel, a typical business
passenger making 10 trips between London and Amsterdam can save
77 percent over the business class fare and 55 percent over the full
economy ticket.[6]

Fare Structure Changes

To begin to cope with the increasing dilution of passenger revenue,
various airlines changed their fare structures. First, it was a small

player—America West—that introduced a fare structure that reduced the top end fares and raised the low end fares. Then, some of the larger airlines began to change fare structure in selected markets—for example, American at Miami, Delta at Cincinnati, US Airways at Philadelphia and Air Canada at Toronto and Montreal. Then Air Canada restructured and simplified their domestic fares completely in 2004. Finally, in January 2005, Delta introduced a new fare structure nationwide—a fare structure that not only addressed the issues of fare irrationality and complexity, but also hoped to slow down the passenger diversion to unconventional airlines. While these changes in pricing strategy are necessary they do not appear to be sufficient to address customer concerns mentioned above. For example, the legacy airlines' top coach fare in US domestic markets is still $499 compared with $299 charged by Southwest Airlines. Moreover, legacy carriers still continue to betray their efforts by continuing to charge the maximum fare in markets where low fare competition has not arrived—an invitation encouraging the unconventional airlines to enter the marketplace and all too visible hypocrisy to customers in those markets.

In Europe, the fare situation is quite a bit different. Almost all unconventional airlines offer one way fares and there are no conditions on fares, other than that they are non-refundable. Moreover, at any one time, there is only one fare available on any one route. However, this fare does increase over time as the date of departure approaches. This scheme does provide an incentive for passengers to book early. Changes are allowed in both itineraries as well as names, but fees for changes can be significant. Conventional airlines do not necessarily follow the same strategy. However, even when conventional airlines sell fares on a roundtrip basis, they still only have one fare in their short haul markets at any given time. British Airways has developed an unusually user friendly website. Rather than attempting to trick passengers into buying a more expensive fare than necessary, on the contrary, the website attempts to point the customer toward the cheapest fare possible.

There is more piece of price-related bad news for the industry. The competitive force that led to a change in the fare structure in domestic markets is beginning to show in international markets. Fares have begun to change in intercontinental markets despite the fact that there are virtually no unconventional airlines offering service. As mentioned in Chapter 2, the competition is only among the old major network airlines and the new smaller network airlines, each competing for its "fair share" of the market. Across the Atlantic, passengers can now purchase much lower fares in business class with an advance purchase. It is only a matter of time until the advance purchase window will decrease or disappear. Even today, with a published business class fare of $5,000 dollars in a market, some passengers are able to buy tickets at $1,700. If the experience of US domestic markets and some intra-Europe markets is any indication of things to come, in five years the prevailing round trip business class fare across the Atlantic could easily be $2,500. Similarly, while a published business class fare between, say, London and Bangkok today is around £5,000 for a nonstop flight, passengers are able to buy tickets at a broad range of fares such as £1,400 on airlines with connecting service within Europe, the Middle East and Asia.

Table 5.2 provides an estimate of the traffic distribution by fare type between New York and London. It is estimated that if everyone paid the same fare, the airline would break even at a fare of about $500. In this example, 60 percent of passengers are paying less than $500 and 40 percent are paying more than $500. Depending on the allocation of costs, some might say that 60 percent of passengers travel at fares that do not cover fully allocated costs and 40 percent travel at fares well above the fully allocated costs. In the past, the cross subsidization worked due to the existence of exceptionally high fares in business class and relatively high unrestricted fares in the economy class. However, if the top-end fares come down there will not be enough revenue. If the top fares come down, the low-end fares need to go up. Consequently, the key to survival is to develop and implement a strategy that improves the traffic mix. The trend, however, appears to be in the other direction. On March 1, 2005, the lowest fare between New York and London was US$206, round trip.

During the winter of 2004/2005 fares have been as low as US$170. While conventional airlines cannot make money on a $200 fare in the winter time, they do make money on the $600-700 fare during the six months from April to September. If new entrants are able to divert these passengers in the summer months, the impact on the incumbents could be fatal. What would be the impact of an unconventional airline based in Europe that operated low fare service with the 380 across the Atlantic in the summer months and between Europe and Asia in the winter months?

Table 5.2 Passenger Distribution by Fare Type: New York-London—An Estimate

Economy Class

Fare	Passengers
$200	10 %
$300	25
$400	20
$500	5
$600	10
$700	5
$800	5
$900	5
$1000	5
Business class	10

Impact Spreads to International Markets

The situation, of course, becomes really serious when one or more unconventional airlines introduce service in intercontinental markets. Unconventional airlines are gaining experience in longer haul markets, both within Europe and in North America (including between the US mainland and the Caribbean). The extent of damage on conventional airlines can be gauged by the experience of jetBlue when it entered selected markets in the Caribbean. The impact on revenue of conventional airlines was dramatic within the first year.[7]

Some executives continue to believe that there is no reason for low fare airlines to enter intercontinental markets since existing airlines already have low fares. Low fares are available on about 10 percent of the seats in the economy cabin. However, while conventional airlines do offer some very low fares, do they make any money on these fares? With an average costs at more than $500 some conventional airlines claim that they can still make money at $200. On the other hand, given the nature of the network business (scheduled services and payload-range capability of intercontinental aircraft), airlines cannot cut out a third of their capacity that does not cover fully allocated costs. Nor can the incumbents cut capacity in different ways such as fly only four days a week in thin business markets. Consequently, given the network nature of scheduled airline service coupled with the existence of extremely low marginal costs, airlines have competed for all traffic, including the really low end. If one offers a $200 fare, rest assured another one will come back with $180.

Some low-cost, low fare airlines will find a way to make service in the intercontinental markets work. It may not be the first one or the second one, but undoubtedly it will happen. It is more likely to happen with a brand new airline than an existing one and one that is purely international rather than one that is domestic. It might be valuable to recall the history within the US domestic markets. When Southwest began to grow beyond its short haul markets, the major US carriers said that they would concentrate on the lucrative transcontinental markets. Southwest could not possibly compete in those markets. Those markets were very different—from the viewpoint of operations, marketing and customer service. The Southwest model could not possibly apply to the US transcontinental markets. Now that jetBlue has succeeded in the US transcontinental markets, the legacy airlines are applying the same logic in intercontinental markets. It will be interesting to see when history will repeat itself.

Based on some simulations on some potential intercontinental routes flown by unconventional airlines, unit costs can be lowered between 25-35 percent, depending on the aircraft flown. A high percentage of the reduction in costs is related to the areas of distribution, and the product—both on the ground and in-flight. Since low fares are already available, market stimulation is limited. Consequently, introduction of service by unconventional airlines will involve a combination of diversion and stimulation. The limited stimulation also means that daily frequency would be limited major markets. The conventional airlines, of course, have the potential to cross subsidize their low fares with the high fares from first and business classes. Moreover, the customer dynamics are very different in short haul vs. long haul intercontinental markets, relating to, for example, the length of stay and the weight given to the fare vs. other travel related expenses.

Coupled with the expansion of low-cost, low fare services on the part of new airlines is the customers' desire for more choice relating to price-service options. The dilemma for airlines in their pricing policies is to discover the revenue/cost balance to provide those choices. Sure the customer wants to find the lowest fare but the customer may also want to pay extra for the aisle seat, or pre-purchase a meal or in-flight entertainment, or purchase other travel related products while making a booking. Customers also want to be able to have a choice of channels and processing systems (for example, self service or personal contact). Again, while providing choices adds to the degree of complexity, the revenue/cost balance must be maintained.

The final element in the pricing strategy relates to the role of branding. Although consumers shopping on the Internet tend to be price-conscious, that is not always the case. In the retail business, it is estimated that only one in three shoppers behaves this way. People do consider brand, ease of site use and their confidence that the product will arrive on time and that the supplier will pay attention to the customer in case of a problem. Why should air travel shoppers be any different? If every online traveler cared only about the price then every reservation would presumably go through low fare websites such as Priceline.com. Some passengers do care about the name of the airline, the type of aircraft, the departure time and the overall brand. Most importantly, there are customers whose loyalty is toward the brand they trust and respect. Consequently, on the positive side, brand does have premium potential, although it varies from region to region. However, there is a negative side also. How much respect is there for an airline that will charge the absolutely highest fare until the day low fare competition arrives, and even then only match fares in the markets where there is competition?

Customer Wants and Needs in Pricing Design

Based on information synthesized through (a) numerous conversations with significant numbers of customers of all types, and (b) extensive research into the body of knowledge from other industries concerning customer behavior, engagement, and expectations, the following points provide some priorities regarding pricing systems within the airline industry.

Clarity and Accessibility

The value equation in place should make sense to the customer. They will understand and accept certain pricing policies pertaining to fare restrictions, time of day, and seasonality, but extreme price swings with no apparent reason should be avoided. The airlines need to build trust and, possibly, use analogues that customers can understand to help explain their pricing policies. Customers can understand the changes in price for certain other perishables (such as fruit), but need to draw the comparison with airline pricing.

Stability

Value pricing, combined with Internet access, means that the customer can actually see what is going on and, at least, attempt to plan accordingly. Passengers need to be able to "see" the fare classes displayed so that they can live with the reality that classes sell. If passengers attempt to get the same fare for travel at a certain time on a certain day, and find the offering changing radically between searches, they lose trust and become suspicious because they do not know what is going on. If, on the other hand, passengers are presented with a menu of different prices and inventories by fare class, it is easy to understand when some become unavailable over time.

Fairness

Passengers simply cannot understand nor accept price ratios of ten times for what appears to be either the same product or one with little difference. They expect and will accept a reasonable ratio between the lowest and the highest fares offered in any given fare class. The airlines must recognize this legitimate need to see ratios changed even if it means bringing the lowest fares up to preserve or create profitability. By the same token, differences due to time of day, day of week, or season of the year need to be seen to be within reasonable bounds.

Flexibility

Flexibility can only come at a price, but again the reason for the difference needs to be visible. If it is more than a service fee due to the inconvenience to the airline for changing a flight reservation, then the reason for the higher fare must be both explainable and defensible. It should not appear punitive.

Accessibility

Passengers like to feel that regardless of the distribution channel they choose they will be treated approximately equally. They do not want to see a huge difference because they are unable or unwilling to use the web. They also do not want to see certain fare classes denied to them because of their choice of channel. They can accept that where it costs an airline more to service them, such as having reservations agents available to them, that there will be a reasonable premium attached to using such services.

Simplicity

The apparently permanent arrival of value pricing in the marketplace after over a decade of false starts signals a new era of simplicity in pricing—largely welcomed by the passenger. The perception of the passenger is that a much smaller numbers of fares are needed to cover the entire range of flexibility that they require, and with which they think the airlines should be able to operate. Should this range be 20 or one half dozen fare classes? However, the differences (in fares) must be accompanied with clearly explainable differences even if they are only "fences" consisting of advanced purchase, length of stay and so forth. In general, the customer does not want to see huge price ratios caused by "fence" differentials. There should be a minimum degree of complexity to respond to the real needs of the marketplace.

Brand Value

Some passengers may attach a premium to the brand of an airline they choose. This will translate that desire into higher prices on that airline or for that particular class of service. However, the passenger now recognizes that with unconventional airlines offering safe, dependable, reasonably priced alternatives to conventional airlines and using clean, modern and comfortable aircraft, that "brand premium" is becoming less. Some passengers claim that some unconventional airlines now, in fact, have superior brands.

Other Price vs. Product Tradeoffs

Passengers will accept certain tradeoffs in exchange for a better price. The most obvious of these is time. The use of multi-stop or connection flights may add a reasonable amount to the total trip time, or may mean shifting to other times of the day, or in some cases, even to different days of the week for those with sufficient flexibility. Again, web access to the various options helps consumers to strike a balance with which they are comfortable. Other product element tradeoffs are less obvious, and need to be carefully planned and managed by airlines, particularly in-flight amenities. This is a case where customer engagement can be very useful to find out exactly what the passenger values and is willing to pay extra for. Finally, the added cost and complexity of delivering these other product elements must be taken into account.

Passenger-Aligned Pricing for Profit Maximization

Obviously, pricing policies must produce a win-win solution both for the passenger and the airlines. As the chapter title indicates, the two major criteria to be taken into consideration are customer satisfaction and sustainable long term profitability. Three important areas to be considered in pricing policies relating to this balance are (a) simplicity-complexity tradeoffs, (b) value-based pricing, and (c) revenue cultivation without increasing costs.

Simplicity-Complexity Tradeoffs

As discussed in Chapter 3, while simplicity is "in" and complexity is "out", the nature of the scheduled airline business, and passengers' desire for choice in price-service options dictates that a certain amount of complexity cannot, and perhaps should not, be eliminated. Just as the simplicity-complexity tradeoff discussion related to network in Chapter 3, and products in Chapter 4, it is now applicable to pricing. Consider the following examples.

- Passengers want to have, and airlines want to produce, service differentiation. But are passengers willing to accept the results? Consider the following question. Would passengers pay more for extra leg room, more desirable seats, more overhead room? Ryanair may have found the answer. They charged for each piece of the flying experience: food, entertainment, extra baggage and so forth. Based on the passenger response, Ryanair decided to end the experiment with the in-flight entertainment. easyJet is reported to be experimenting with charging for early boarding. As discussed in Chapter 2, the trend appears to be a la carte pricing.

- Revenue management in the past focused on analyses of what customers bought rather than what they wanted to buy—a system based on history rather than actual preference. For example, revenue management took into consideration such factors as how many passengers bought tickets in each fare class and at what price, not recognizing that their own system of offers was responsible for the outcome. How different might things have been if there had been only three, less disparate fares offered?

- Major network airlines operating in a broad spectrum of global markets perceive the need to change fares frequently based on many factors, such as a hypercompetitive environment, a perishable product, lack of genuine product differentiation, the network aspect of the business, extremely low marginal costs, fluctuating foreign exchange rates, and extremely variable demand—by season, route and market. Is the complexity of the system appropriate, or justified?

- Competitive fares do not mean identical fares. Differentiation, even in a commodity market, has benefits and rewards. It is unlikely that most passengers consider the experience of a Southwest flight identical to that of jetBlue. But the cost of differentiation must not exceed the added value that passengers perceive. What really does the passenger want? If it is choice and differentiation then the airline may have to become even more complex but that complexity must have clear financial benefits to the airline. Added complexity that does not generate premiums is unaffordable.

To answer the simplicity-complexity questions and to design the optimal pricing structure requires greater understanding of how to provide value to targeted customers. Such an understanding (for example, the desire for and the degree of a la carte pricing) can only be obtained from the deployment of such techniques as customer engagement, discussed in Chapter 1. The complexity and irrationality of the fare structure experienced by passengers is the result of the following factors.

- The airline industry had a unique distribution system—resulting partly from the availability of global distribution systems described in the next chapter—that enabled airlines to change their fares several times a day, resulting in a very unstable fare structure.

- Instead of using technology to simplify the fare structure, airlines capitalized on the availability of technology (for example, revenue management systems with more than two dozen booking classes) to carry price discrimination to its ultimate level.

- Airlines had access to a unique system of submitting fares to a special organization that collected and collated fares from all participating airlines and then sold the information back to each airline. This system enabled airlines not only to see the reaction of competitors to a proposed change but also to match fares of competitors. Airlines did not just replace their fares with those of competitors but simply added to them. So if one airline had 30 fares in a market and a competitor introduced five new ones, the first airline kept its 30 fares and added the competitors' five fares.

- The airline business is extremely low margin and therefore every percent of additional revenue matters. So, if an airline can take advantage of a change in exchange rates, for example, between the British pound and the American dollar, there is a temptation to introduce differential fares—a decision that adds complexity.

In the final analysis, simplicity has tradeoffs. If the passenger wants choices and differentiation then the airline may have to become even more complex if it means introducing different services for different people. Nevertheless, from a passenger viewpoint the services offered must give the appearance of simplicity even though it means greater sophistication from the airline's viewpoint to address the additional functions to be taken care of in the back office.

Value-Based Pricing

American Airlines tried to implement value pricing more than a decade ago but the other airlines did not go along with it. The structure was implemented for a short period of time, it triggered a fare war, there were heavy losses and the US industry abandoned it. Now the environment has changed sufficiently that airlines are now willing to experiment with the concept. It is interesting to contemplate what would have happened if the US industry had adopted the value pricing proposed by American Airlines in 1992. Would the unconventional airlines have become as great as they have become? It is doubtful that unconventional airlines would have been so successful without the segmented fare structure, encompassing the degree of unfairness perceived by consumers.

Being competitive does not mean being identical. It depends on consumers' perception of value. If an airline competes in a market where it is the only one with a nonstop, then it does not need to match the entire fare structure of a competitor offering only connecting service. But, it should not gouge either. However, in markets where the services are identical, airlines do have to match because the differences among the airlines are relatively small. Some examples of airlines that try to sell on "value" include Southwest, Lufthansa, and Virgin Atlantic. In the case of Southwest, for example, its value proposition does not include product features such as assigned seats, two class service, meals, or access to airport lounges. Instead its value proposition is partly measurable as a lower price—a top fare of $299 vs. $499—and partly emotional—knowing that you are not getting gouged, even if the fare may be a few dollars higher in some markets. In the case of Lufthansa, it is consistency and reliability. In the case of Virgin, it is the fulfillment of the expectations associated with the brand—value. These intangible benefits can and have deterred some passengers from going to competitors even if competitors offered lower fares, but only as long as the differential was reasonable.

Revenue Cultivation

Figure 4.10 in the previous chapter showed that despite all the cost reduction efforts by the conventional airlines, there is still a significant difference between the unit operating cost of the conventional and the unconventional airlines. It is doubtful that major legacy carriers can get their costs down to the level of low-cost airlines. Perhaps, they should not even try. Rather, the objective instead should be to restore a CASM-RASM equilibrium within acceptable percentage ranges. The keys are, first, the need for integration and consistency within and between different marketing elements, and second, a clear customer affirmation of any price differential. If one assumes that the legacy major airlines must live with an unfavorable cost differential then they need to persuade their passengers to pay a premium to reflect the preferred product elements.

The premium is decreasing particularly as it relates to the loyalty aspect. Frequent flyer programs have not only added an enormous liability for some carriers but passengers are experiencing more difficulty in taking advantage of the rewards. Consider just one example of upgrades. With a reduction in the fare differential between first and economy class fares within the US domestic market, there are considerably less seats available for upgrades. Moreover, with premium class service now available on some low fare airlines, the value of an upgrade is less on legacy airlines. Consider another potentially conflicting strategy. Some airlines may consider limiting the number of local passengers on a domestic segment due to the low fares in the marketplace and concentrating on the higher margin passengers making connections to international flights. This theory would work except that it would force the airline to reduce the frequency to align the capacity with the international demand. A reduction in frequency would then result in a reduction in the premium that the airline assumed, resulting from the availability of high frequency. Consequently, there is a need to identify pricing policies that are cross functionally integrated and that can help to cultivate revenue without producing a comparable increase in costs.

Consider the data shown in Table 5.1 above regarding transatlantic fares. Depending on the airline and the season, load factors for paying passengers in first class can range from 15-25 percent, in business class from 40 to 60 percent, and in the economy class from 65 to 85 percent. These numbers represent load factors computed on the basis of paying passengers, not upgrades or airline staff traveling for free or at highly discounted fares. How could load factors be improved with paying passengers? One answer could be to control upgrades. There are cases where passengers have purchased tickets from the lowest fare class for $200, paid an upgrade fee of $800 round trip, essentially purchasing a business class seat for $1,000. The same seat would retail for over $5,000 and produce, even on a net fare basis, revenue in excess of $3,000. Airlines are just beginning to think about restricting the upgrade to tickets of, say, at least, $1,000 price. However, such a pricing policy needs substantial cross functional coordination and discipline. Undoubtedly, the executive in charge of the frequent flyer program is likely to be against such a pricing decision, arguing that such a policy would drive away the airline's most valued customers.

The key need is to drill down deep into customer profitability, both from the revenue side as well as from the cost side. Although it appears to be possible to look at the profitability of each customer (exemplified by the experience of some major banks in the UK and Canada), one could concentrate, say, on just the top 5 percent. For example, Figure 5.4 shows that 5 percent of this airline's customers generate 25 percent of the revenue—the two bars on the right hand side of the chart. For one major airline, the top 10 percent of the passengers generated 60 percent of the revenue and almost 100 percent of the profitability. It is the detailed examination of these 5-10 percent of passengers to see how an airline might generate more revenue or decrease its costs that will determine the profitability of these segments.

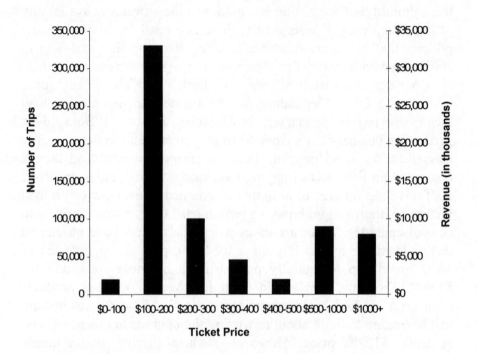

Figure 5.4 Distribution of Passenger Trips by Fare Level

We could start, for example, investigating the distribution of the trips generated by this 5 percent of the passengers in Figure 5.4 that generated 25 percent of the revenue. In this case, Figure 5.5 shows the distribution of these 5 percent of the passengers by the number of trips they make. The number of trips ranges from less than six to more than 24 per year. This is an example of drilling down to explore revenue sources. Ultimately, it is the availability of detailed, relevant, and timely information that will allow an airline to make better decisions.[8] This is one area where some conventional airlines have competitive strength. They not only possess the necessary raw information, they possess the techniques, systems, and skills to drill down into passenger behavior to develop pricing policies that satisfy passengers and at the same time improve their profitability.

Next, consider the changing role of revenue management. Assuming that airlines will continue to lose the edge of using fare rules to differentiate between fare categories, and the convergence

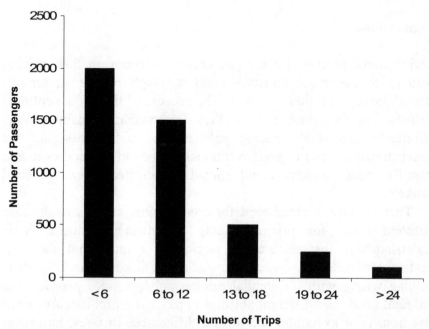

Figure 5.5 Distribution of Passengers by the Number of Trips

between the top fares and the low fares, what is the optimal number of fare classes and the price differential among the various classes? This optimization must take into consideration additional revenue generated on the one hand and the customer complaints discussed above on the other hand.

Pricing policies can help an airline to cultivate revenue but the process requires cross functional integration, discipline, long term orientation, sophisticated methods for data warehousing and mining, and above all genuine customer orientation. While these statements may seem to be extremely obvious, there is some evidence that some airlines are not practicing even the obvious. In the US, airlines share basic data. It is not uncommon to see a situation in which when one airline finds out that its load factor is 3 percent below its competitor, the executive order comes down to increase the load factor by selling more seats at deeply discounted fares—regardless of the long term impact.

Conclusions

Conventional airlines did not pay enough attention in their pricing policies to passenger concerns until the high paying passengers started abandoning their services. The success of the unconventional airlines can be attributed to their reasonable, understandable, affordable, and stable pricing policies. The traffic losses of the conventional airlines to unconventional airlines in US domestic and intra-European markets could spread to selected intercontinental markets.

There is now a clear need for conventional airlines to develop different skills for pricing. Being a network business, it is understandable that differential pricing is a must, but the new environment calls for a better management of discount fares. There is nothing wrong with differential pricing policies since people have different needs and different abilities to pay. The problem arises not just from poor execution and absurd differences in fares, but, most importantly, from forcing the customer to adapt to the fare rather than developing a fare to adapt to the passenger. Although eliminating the fences has diluted the yield for conventional airlines, they must now find innovative ways to link the pricing policies with the product architecture, for example, along the lines suggested in Figure 4.5 in the previous chapter.

Notes

[1]   Fares checked on the website of US Airways in April 19, 2005 for next day travel and with no restrictions.

[2] It should be pointed out that the market between JFK Airport, New York and Heathrow Airport, London is unique with respect to its size and composition of traffic. Premium cabin fares in other transatlantic markets are much lower. For example, business class fares (comparable to the data shown in Table 5.1) from JFK, New York to Zurich, Paris and Madrid are about $6,800, $6,300, and $4,700, respectively.

[3] Producers of multiple products can allocate their fixed costs to the final product prices in inverse proportion to the price elasticity of demand (Ramsey pricing).

[4] Kumar, Nirmalya, *Marketing as Strategy: Understanding the CEO's Agenda for Driving Growth and Innovation* (Boston, MA: Harvard Business School Press, 2004), p. 37.

[5] Mason, Keith J. "The Value and usage of ticket flexibility for short haul business travelers", Presentation at the Eighth Air Transport Research Society Conference, Istanbul and reported in Mason, Keith J., "Observations of fundamental changes in the demand for aviation services", *Journal of Air Transport Management*, Volume 11 (2005), p. 23.

[6] Mason, Keith J., "Observations of fundamental changes in the demand for aviation services," *Journal of Air Transport Management*, Volume 11 (2005), p. 23.

[7] jetBlue's strategy to test various markets is evident from its entry and exit in the Santa Domingo market. The carrier presumably found out that some markets are not ready for the kind of low-cost, low fare services offered by such carriers. The market was heavily ethnic with heavy preference, for example, for the traditional agency distribution channel rather than dealing directly with the airline. Other differences include exceptionally large amounts of baggage, and a significant directional market as well as seasonality.

[8] Hurd, Mark and Nyberg, Lars, *The Value Factor: How Global Leaders Use Information for Growth and Competitive Advantage*, (Princeton, NJ: Bloomberg Press, 2004), p. 49.

Chapter 6

Exploiting Distribution Diversity

Aside from the desperate need to reduce and control costs, there are three major forces bringing about significant change in the landscape of the distribution chain.

- Changing behavior of leisure and business passengers (desire for value, choice and willingness to buy online, and acceptance of the products and services offered by the unconventional airlines).

- Expansion of technology (the Internet, search engines, web-based global distribution systems) that enable airlines to offer value-based products and services to passengers.

- Deregulation in the United States of the GDSs enabling them to change their business models.

These forces are inter-dependent. For example, one reason unconventional airlines have been so successful is because technology (the Internet) enables them to distribute their products in a much more cost effective way.

This chapter discusses these three major forces and how they are impacting (a) the business models of two members of the distribution chain—agents and the GDSs, and their relationship with airlines, and (b) the distribution strategies of airlines. Just as consumers' desires for greater price-service options and the governments' liberalization of the regulatory policies led to the development and phenomenal expansion of unconventional airlines, now similar trends are forcing the two major members of the distribution chain—agents and

GDSs—to realign their business models to adapt to the realities of the changing marketplace. These changes, in turn, are providing an opportunity for airlines—both conventional and unconventional—to capitalize on the diversity of distribution to reduce costs and regain control of distribution of products, but also to present to customers clear value propositions.[1]

Major Forces Impacting Airline Distribution

Passengers

Technologies Driving Choice   As every chapter has pointed out, customers want choice. Some want to find the lowest fare. Others, however, may want the option to pay extra for more desirable seat locations while they are booking the airline ticket on an airline website. Customers should be able to have a choice of channels and processing systems (self service or personal contact). Some want to cross shop all airlines and not be restricted to the offers made by one airline where, for example, in international markets one carrier may have limited service. Consider some examples of the choices leisure and corporate travelers need.

Leisure passengers want flexibility in how they search for flights online. Orbitz exploited this desire by allowing consumers to search not just for specific days of travel, but to also search for weekend trips in a given month. Meta-search site Kayak created a Flash-based fare display page that allows consumers to see the tradeoffs between flight times and fares.[2] Flash minimizes the time-consuming page reloading process. In a non-Flash website, a consumer clicks, the information is sent back to the website, and the webpage re-loads. This is how most web pages work—consumers click, then wait for something to happen. With Flash, all the information is loaded into the background of the web page. The page changes instantly when a consumer clicks on a web page in Flash. The benefit to consumers is that they can alter their choices (say, the dates of a trip) and have the results displayed instantly.

On the hotel side, iHotelier's 1-Click a Flash-based booking system (for an example, see www.broadmoor.com), allows consumers to quickly see the tradeoffs between dates, room type and price. These systems mirror the interaction between consumers and offline travel agents, where consumers are quickly given tradeoffs between attributes of the product they are booking. Flash allows these tradeoffs to be seen on one webpage, a giant leap forward from the constant back-and-forth currently required to understand these tradeoffs.

Turning to corporate travel passengers, large corporations are interested in consolidating bookings from around the globe. It could be valuable for corporate online booking solutions such as Sabre's GetThere and Amadeus' e-Travel to resemble consumer agency sites, such as Travelocity and Expedia. The user interface on corporate tools can be cumbersome and may discourage corporate travelers. Since each of the tools is owned by a GDS, they could take cues from their online counterparts to improve the usability of the sites. Improved usability can lead to increased usage of these tools by travelers, leading to greater cost savings and better control of travel expenditures. This ease of use is exemplified by the corporate travel products offered by Expedia and Orbitz.

Leisure and Business Blurs   It is important to note that it is becoming more difficult to ascertain the differences between leisure and business travelers, as the lines between the two segments continue to blur. Recall the examples discussed in Chapter 1 of the needs of different travelers. However, regardless of whether a consumer is traveling for leisure or business, the vast majority are concerned about paying a fair price. As discussed in the previous chapter, the complex fare structure has left consumers bewildered and frustrated when they begin their research for a trip. Online distributors—both airline websites and travel agencies—responded to this confusion by marketing their sites as being the one place where consumers can find the lowest fares. Unfortunately, consumers quickly found that there is no one website with the lowest fares. Because of the inherent complexity in fares and distribution structures, each distribution channel will sometimes have the lowest fares while occasionally offering higher fares.

For example, one website may restrict its search very tightly around the stated departure time whereas another website may explore departures far from the desired time of departure. This latitude produces lower fares on websites that use a broader time span and leads the consumer to assume (incorrectly) that this particular website offers lower fares. An online agency can also use different rules to create itineraries with lower fares by using less convenient connections—again creating confusion in the mind of the consumer that some websites offer lower fares than other websites. The end result is that consumers have little faith that they can limit their research to one website and feel compelled to visit multiple websites before purchasing an airline ticket.

Consequently, consumers aside, even airlines appear to be frustrated with their efforts to convince consumers that they have the lowest fares and that the consumer does not need to go to other websites. Would a guarantee by an airline that it offers the lowest fare discourage a price-conscious passenger from visiting other websites or, in fact, provide encouragement? What if every airline offered the same guarantee? Does the airline offer the lowest fare all the time or some of the time? That is the difference between airlines such as Southwest and retailers such as Wal-Mart who offer everyday low prices. While it is possible that Southwest or Wal-Mart may have a slightly higher price on some flight or some item on some day, customers feel secure that they are not being gouged. They have comfort in knowing that they are always getting a reasonable price even if it is not the lowest price.

Price-Service Tradeoffs   It is interesting to note that suppliers often think that shoppers on the Internet looking for hard goods focus only on price. While online shoppers definitely take price into consideration, they also consider the brand, ease of site use, and some confidence that the product will arrive on time and that the supplier will pay attention to the customer in case of a problem such as damaged goods. Why should air travel shoppers be any different?

Some passengers do care about the name of the airline, the type of aircraft, the departure time, and the overall brand.

While airlines have relied on often-copied lowest fare guarantees and bonus miles to drive consumer behavior, they have missed opportunities to build trust with consumers through their websites. Consumer trust can be built with transparency of information and an understandable fare structure. The new fare initiative introduced in the US by Delta in January 2005 has helped move the industry toward understandable pricing policies. Now, airlines should couple the new fares with redesigned websites that focus on building consumer trust and offering them greater control over the booking process.

Improving functionality for the passenger   The following are some examples of areas that would improve functionality of travel websites.

1. Simplification and Rationality of the Fare Structure. Presumably, as mentioned in the previous chapter, passengers would feel more comfortable in making their choices if they knew that there were only a half dozen types of fares with a reasonable and a rational spread. Just as it was pointed out in the previous chapter, ordinary people have difficulty understanding why fares would be higher in short haul markets than in long haul markets or why fares would be the same for travel on nonstop flights vs. flights that make a connection and involve a long layover.

2. Greater Transparency in the Fare Structure. Passengers would feel more comfortable if they knew the differences between fares in different fare classes and the availability of those fares. Southwest and Air Canada have displays that show consumers the price and benefit differences between fare classes. Wouldn't a passenger take a seat if that passenger knew that there was only one seat left rather than take the risk and shop at other websites? From a different perspective, a passenger may decide not to take a particular flight if it is "packed"—a decision that may certainly not be in the interest of the airline.

3. Display of Competitive Fares. If airlines know that consumers will search around for information on competitive fares, is it not better to provide that information in the first place? Since the Internet has brought about transparency, airlines could take advantage of it instead of fighting it. If an online agency provides information on competitive fares why could not an individual airline do the same? In fact, why should the airline stop at only providing the information on fares on competitive traditional airlines? How about providing information on low fare airlines, to the extent that information is available?

4. Adequate Information to Make Tradeoffs. Passengers need to understand tradeoffs between alternate cities, days of week, times of day and fare class—just as the information would be available from an agent. If customers do not see what they want, they leave. If there appears to be a problem and mistrust starts to take place then customers leave and may not return.

5. More Information for Window Shoppers. Some online websites have begun to improve in this area. For example, there are now websites where a passenger can see low fares to a variety of destinations from the passenger's home base—for example, those passengers who want to get away for a few days, to a warm destination. Some websites also provide virtual tours of their premium cabins. Although some permit this already, all airlines could even allow passengers to hold reservations for 24 hours just as they allow through their call centers.

6. Some Degree of Personalization. Although some airlines do provide seat maps, the process could be improved, by pointing out the best and the worst locations of seats by aircraft type. Since consumers can already get this information by visiting Seatguru.com, airlines should also be making this information available on their websites. Discounts could be offered on the worst seats. Who knows some extremely price conscious passengers might even look for the worst seats? Why hide information on the quality of seats? Since there are ways for passengers to find out this information, why not

make it readily available? The airline forthcoming with all the information may in fact become the most trusted airline.

7. Ability to Control the Content. Could airlines not develop systems that allow passengers to slice the data in any way they want and to search the fares how they want, and to understand the tradeoffs between various aspects of the ticket price and the associated restrictions? The Flash tools described above allow hotel bookers to determine similar tradeoffs. Although airlines have done a reasonable job in providing content they have not provided customers with ways to control the content. As some experts say the Internet is a great channel for providing information only if the person knows what the person is looking for. The Internet is not that user friendly for people who do not know what they are looking for, such as those looking for a beach or ski getaway.

8. Credibility. Some airline websites lack credibility. It is not comforting if a passenger finds the availability of only full fares on an airline's website and accidentally happens to see lower fares on another website. One of the most frustrating experiences is for an airline's website to show a low fare that is not available. Some search engines create non-traditional routings that are not available through standard websites.

Technology

The four primary areas of expanding technology having a fundamental impact on airline distribution are (1) airline websites, (2) web-based engines for search and booking (3) the development of alternative web-based GDSs and (4) the introduction of so-called Meta Search engines, such as Kayak. These developments in technology have helped airlines undertake direct distribution, consumers have some price-service options, and online agents to enter the marketplace.

These new technologies have already affected the relationship between travel suppliers and consumers. For example, the new web-based GDSs may affect consumers directly if distributors using the technology pass on the cost savings. In addition, each of these technologies places more information in consumers' hands and moves control of the transaction from the airline or travel agent squarely onto the consumer. As seen from the discussion of these technologies, consumers have embraced these changes, rewarding airlines and related businesses that have embraced them to the greatest degree.

Direct Distribution   As stated in the previous chapter, unconventional airlines' success has been attributed not just to the availability of low fares but also to the low cost and ease of product distribution. Most unconventional airlines rely heavily on direct distribution, although there is some variation within the industry. Consider, for example, the distribution channels of Southwest, jetBlue, Independence Air and Ryanair. Until recently both Southwest and jetBlue participated in a traditional GDS—Sabre. Ryanair initially participated in four GDSs. Southwest generated 12 percent of its revenue through the GDS and 60 percent through its own website while jetBlue generated 75 percent of its revenue through its own website. Consequently, at the beginning of 2005, jetBlue—an airline with a strong brand name—decided to withdraw from the traditional GDS. In the case of Ryanair—an airline with a strong passenger following—the airline pulled out of all four GDSs. Independence Air, a new airline that had flown previously as a feeder to United chose to use the services of a GDS but only on a menu based pricing system—pay for the services needed, and only after trying to avoid the GDSs altogether.[3] While it is true that unconventional airlines have simple itineraries, less complex hub-and-spoke systems, and little-to-no international travel, one could assume that they benefit significantly less from the services provided by traditional GDSs. This is true for some unconventional airlines such as jetBlue and Southwest. However, others such as AirTran, Spirit, and Frontier do rely on traditional GDSs to varying extents, especially when trying to break into a new market.

As a whole, airlines in Europe have gone further and faster on direct distribution than airlines in the US. For example, online bookings for easyJet and Ryanair are around the 95 percent level, with no access to travel agents. For the remaining 5 percent, in the case of Ryanair, the bookings go through the airline's call centers. However, not only is there a premium cost for the phone call but the call center is not open on weekends. In Asia, the distribution channel mix is quite different. For example, because very few people have credit cards, the unconventional airlines are selling their products through 7-11 stores who have established accounts with certain banks. Nevertheless, the trend (for the ultra low-cost, low fare airlines), is still to find ways to avoid the traditional agents.

Just as airlines embraced their websites for the cost savings they provided, most airlines initially embraced online agencies for the lower distribution costs they provided. However, many airlines found that over time these lower distribution costs came with their own set of problems, including (a) dilution in yield and (b) a potential loss in control. In some cases, airlines discovered that some online agencies did not in fact turn out to be as low cost as envisioned, and produced lower yield than their own websites. This situation occurred because online agencies integrated technologies (such as ITA Software) that offered consumers a wider range of low fares than the airlines' own websites were capable of finding. In addition, Orbitz focused on creating a fare display that offered a wide array of low fares from which consumers could choose. These initiatives initially attracted consumers who were focused on low fares and little else, much to the detriment of yield.

Hotels faced the same issue, but even more painfully, in 2002, as they ceded control and margins to third-party distributors through the so-called merchant model arrangements. Just as quickly, though, hotels reigned in these deals, forbidding individual properties from making deals with third parties, eliminating loyalty program benefits from third-party bookings, and instructing front-desk staff to all-but-reprimand third-party bookers for their choice of booking channel. These changes have been extremely effective in driving traffic to hotel chains' websites at the expense of third-party distributors. Airlines have powerful weapons in gate agents and flight attendants and should be using them to explain the benefits of booking on the airline's website and drawbacks of third-party distributors. Some airlines already use an in-flight video to explain the benefits of booking on their websites and have flight attendants promote their frequent flyer programs. Airlines could also have flight attendants announce website benefits. Some hotels have asked their front desk staff to inform customers about the drawbacks of booking on third-party websites and they have observed a noticeable shift in customer behavior since this initiative. Airline agents could do the same.

Agencies—Online and Offline Despite the lower yield and less cost reduction than envisioned, airlines continue to evaluate the powerful online channels, at least in the short term. Independence Air found third-party distributors beneficial after an attempt to distribute only through its own website—a move that did not result in sufficient load factors. Most conventional airlines, though, will find that their distribution needs will include online agencies because of their reach. The entrance of four big-name search engines will bring mutual benefits to airlines and customers—AOL, Google, MSN and Yahoo.

There is also the consideration of the growing ability of online agencies to shift share on a route-by-route basis. Online agencies allow airlines to do targeted marketing based on where a consumer is traveling. For example, an agency can display a targeted advertisement for a traveler flying airline A, in a particular market, promoting the airline's service in this market. Moreover, online agencies are able to bias the results page so that an airline's flights receive better placement than the competitor's flights. Those marketing tools can help give the first airline a boost on the particular route. Airlines will find that the benefits offered by the agency may, at least, equal the costs associated with the channel.

While online agencies have historically focused on price-sensitive leisure travelers, since 2003 they have increased their focus on the lucrative corporate travel market. Products such as Orbitz for Business, Travelocity Business and Expedia Corporate Travel have gained traction in the past year and will continue to thrive in the small-to-mid-sized market, especially if they are (a) customer-friendly and (b) trustworthy. These products would also be of interest to those larger corporations that are far more price sensitive than service sensitive. However, corporations that are more sensitive to service, especially for their senior executives, will continue to rely on traditional offline agents or require an executive desk staffed around the clock.

Given the interest of large companies in both price sensitivity for some travelers and service sensitivity for others, some large offline agencies are offering both a lower cost option as well as a higher cost option. The revenue generated for conventional airlines through online agencies is still very low—less than 15 percent in most cases. This is interesting in that the low-cost online agencies were supposed to have reduced the conventional airlines' reliance on travel agents. Instead the airlines have become captive to a few online agencies. Even worse, online agencies are selling based simply on price where offline agencies generally sell on value. Yet, if the major purchase criterion is price through online agencies, how can an airline market its points of differentiation, such as a higher seat pitch? This is an example of how an agent can make a big difference pointing out that a carrier has higher seat pitch or is more likely to take care of the passenger in case of irregular operations. Thus, fees paid to agents, now in a different form than the original commissions, may make perfect sense for some carriers in some markets.

Technology that makes fares transparent forces airlines to lower fares resulting in a reduction in yield. Before the availability of search engines, the search for lower fares was conducted mostly by leisure travelers as neither the business traveler nor the agent had the time to go searching through lots of sites to find out the lower fare. Typically, a business traveler would call an agent and the agent would quote the fare. Alternatively, a business traveler using a corporate online booking tool like Sabre's GetThere would look at the available fare but could certainly not employ the search engines now available to review all available fares. Consequently, the expansion of technology is having a significant impact on the fares used by business travelers. Technology has also enabled an airline to hold back preferred content from traditional channels and make it available for its own website. The inability of offline agents to have access to all the content of an airline reduced their competitiveness, causing them to look for alternative ways of obtaining the preferred content.

The main weakness of online agencies is their inability to make recommendations based on criteria other than low price—a clear strength of offline agencies. Those offline agents who are clearly differentiating themselves from others who are simple ticket sellers can benefit by offering advice through their expertise. The Internet is perfect for selling a customer something that the customer wants—a low fare ticket between New York and London next Tuesday. However, online agencies are inefficient at figuring out what a customer really needs. The online agency does not know the true needs of the customer or the personality of the customer or the experience of the customer with a particular product or service. The offline agent does or at least can learn this behavior or personality. Therefore, in some ways online agencies are nothing more than GDSs with a reasonably friendly customer front end. They cannot possibly make recommendations based on individual customer preferences. Although online agencies have tried to improve their products by offering recommendations, they have had limited success.

Fee Structures The market will continue to be segmented in the foreseeable future. Tickets will still be booked offline given the complexity of travel—particularly international travel or travel requiring recommendations. However, for simple travel—such as in some US domestic or intra-European markets—the online channel offers sufficient service. The agency business model will converge, for example, as some offline agents are now offering online services and some online agencies are using their technology to offer offline agent type of customer service. A large offline agent's clerk may well say to a customer, "OK if you want just a straight ticket, 5 dollars, if your company wants a report, another 10 dollars, if you want an agent to pick up the phone and talk with you, 15 more dollars". Some technology help desks are reported to charge by the minute. Similarly, online agencies offer business travelers the ability to make their online booking with a travel agent for a small fee.

The Impact of Search Engines In the first half of 2005, the industry has been abuzz with the possibilities offered by so called Meta

Search engines, such as Kayak, Sidestep and Mobissimo. These companies do not sell airline tickets; rather they search multiple sellers of tickets (agencies and airlines' websites) and then send the customer directly to whichever site the customer chooses. For the most part, online agencies have decided not to participate with the Meta Search companies, claiming that they already perform air fare searches. However, many airlines have embraced this new technology because, while they pay a small fee for each ticket sold, the booking actually occurs on the airline's website. While it remains to be seen whether these companies will build enough momentum to succeed, they provide a way for airlines to reduce their distribution costs associated with very price-conscious customers.

Another new technology is emerging that also could lower distribution costs for airlines. Based on web technology and desktop computers, new web-based GDSs represent very low-cost alternatives to the existing GDSs. As with any new system, the viability of the current systems is being questioned in such areas as:

- Depth and breadth of content.

- Ability to handle large volumes.

- True costs.

- Channel management functionality and support.

- Need to change business processes.

- Application in other regions of the world.

Airlines are clearly interested in evaluating the viabilities of these technologies since their ticket costs using the existing GDSs are estimated to range between US$7 and US$16. Despite the first generation characteristics of these technologies, some airlines have already begun to encourage agencies to use the new systems through financial and content incentives. In due course, these systems could become more sophisticated—for example, being able to provide interline capability, rebook cancelled flights, handle complex itineraries, cancel tickets, issue refunds, exchange tickets and provide passenger profiles. On the positive side, the new generation of GDSs uses the web to store, search and retrieve information on fares instead of on mainframes, resulting in faster searches. Secondly, these systems are exclusively technical connectors between suppliers and distributors. There is no economic relationship between the supplier and the distributor.

Despite the aforementioned benefits, it would take a lot to persuade agents to switch from the traditional GDSs to the new systems for the following reasons.

- The traditional systems offer greater functionality than the first generation low-cost GDSs.

- Agents have familiarity with the use of existing systems, providing a comfort level.

- The traditional GDSs provide substantial economic incentives for agents to use those systems.

- The traditional GDSs have reduced their costs making it less attractive for airlines to consider the adoption of new forms of GDS.

- Besides a general reduction in prices, some GDSs, led by Amadeus, are moving toward pricing systems based on value. This trend is likely to proliferate.

Finally, technology can now facilitate an enormous expansion of dynamic packaging which previously had been restricted to the leisure segment but could now produce desirable customized products for the business segment, including an increase in the use of passenger profiles relating to travel preferences and preferred modes of communications.

Deregulation

At the end of 2003, the US Department of Transportation decided to lift all regulations relating to GDSs. The two critical constraints were (a) that GDSs refrain from biasing flight listings in favor of some airlines to the disadvantage of others, and (b) that an airline must provide all of its fares to GDSs. The primary changes since deregulation are that GDSs can now charge airlines for better placement in the page where fares are displayed to travel agents, and that airlines have greater latitude in what fares they choose to distribute through a given GDS. For example, an airline flying a new route can pay a certain GDS to be listed first for flight searches in that new city. This benefits both the GDS, who earns income from this arrangement, and the airline, who receives direct value from the GDS's wide reach. As discussed below, deregulation of the GDS industry is certainly leading to the development of new business models.

Observing the winds of change in airline distribution, traditional GDSs began to change their business models quite early, exemplified by the following initiatives.

- Sabre's decision to create its own online portal (Travelocity).

- Sabre's offer of its Direct Connect Availability Three-Year Option (DCA3)—discounts of 10-15 percent in GDS booking fees by segment for three years in exchange for the availability of all fares (including the low fares available normally on an airline's own website).

- Amadeus, which purchased a stake in the European online travel website Opodo, introduced its value-pricing initiative in which it offered a fee structure based on where the reservation is made and how the ticket is sold rather than a flat fee per transaction system—in other words, higher fees for higher value reservations and volumes.

- Cendant's—the owner of Galileo—decision to acquire Orbitz (the travel site owned and developed by US major airlines), the UK wholesaler Gullivers Travel (an owner of an online travel agency), and the European travel website ebookers.

The aforementioned initiatives are just the beginning of the process to examine the viability of the traditional GDSs. The traditional GDSs represent technology that is more than 30 years old. Although they have offered add-on newer technology interfaces, the systems are inefficient relative to today's technology and expensive to maintain. Their fee structure, which involves charging airlines for distribution and paying an incentive to travel agents for making a booking, is not viable for the current airline situation. New GDSs offer an appealing price structure to airlines because they offer lower costs than traditional GDSs and they do not pay travel agents an incentive.

The main area of focus of the new business models of traditional GDSs are in the following areas:

- A menu driven price-service structure in which the services provided are un-bundled to enable an airline to select and pay for the services needed.

- New value-adding information such as profiles of the passenger making the reservation, filings of competitive fares, closure of certain fare classes, identification of situations where ticket time limits are not being enforced and the status of flight coupons.

- Moving away from being pure order takers and processors of transactions to order makers within the framework of (a) the emerging models of suppliers and (b) changing behavior of customers so as to not just add but drive value in the travel chain.

- Reducing not just transaction costs but overall costs, for example, through an increase in the use of e-tickets that not only lower the cost of ticket distribution, but also provide an improvement in accounting and billing.

- A value adding fee structure based, for example, on the GDS reach (exposure) and reservation yield.

Deregulation of the GDSs now allows their owners to develop and implement market-based practices, relating, for example, to pricing strategies, content access, contract terms and conditions, and products and services based on different technologies. Examples include engines that search for lower fares on alternate dates and alternate airports (improving the look-to-book ratio), corporate focused booking tools (providing greater business flexibility and control), and technology services that facilitate self service. Value adding features of emerging technology include not only the improvement of core functionality (reissuing of tickets, partial refunds, exchanges, and so forth) but also making back office functions more efficient, pulling in and pushing out more efficiently customer relationship management oriented information (from customers to agents to airlines and back to customers), and making communications and interactions among the disparate systems easier and less costly.

The pending deregulation relating to GDSs in Europe is likely to have similar impact on the industry as in the case of the United States. The extent of changes will depend on which rules the European regulators throw out and which they keep.[4]

What Customers Want from the Distribution System

GDSs typically have thought of travel agents as their end user. However, since the advent of the Internet, the situation has changed from the viewpoint of consumers. Although consumers do not know (or care) about how fare and schedule information is compiled, their choices are very much affected by distribution technologies. Given that, it is imperative that airlines work together with traditional GDSs and new generation GDSs to create a product that meets consumer needs. As explained in the previous chapter about the sources of information, following are some examples of elements that will create an optimal consumer booking experience.

Control

Passengers want a sense that they have some control over their own travel plans, and that they are not being manipulated. They want a system that puts reasonable limits on their plans in exchange for price and service features.

Credibility and Trust

Passengers want a sense of trust that what they are being told is what is actually happening. If an airline promises that the lowest fare is always available on their own web site, then they should not be able to find lower fares by other means such as web based search engines.

Ease of Access and Use

The chosen channel should be accessible and easy to use. If it is web based, the degree of complexity in the site should be chosen with great care, trading off complexity versus simplicity based on clearly demonstrated preferences by the passenger. It is possible that there may be a need for two channels—one just for reservations and another which also includes a full service menu of seat selection, description of on-board amenities, aircraft seat charts, airport descriptions and so forth. Many passengers still want the ability to work with an agent because of complexity of itinerary or service requirements, a lack of comfort with computers, corporate guidelines, or other reasons. If surcharges are to be levied, they should be seen to be fair.

Engagement and Loyalty Considerations

As systems evolve, passengers want to be consulted about the new directions taken. For example, the use of Flash technology in the new

Meta Search systems means the potential for more passenger options and faster turnaround, but such innovations should reflect passenger needs, and not be technology driven. Loyalty programs are often developed and managed separately from reservations systems. Passengers are often frustrated by this separation, as they want to see the acquisition and cashing in of rewards as a seamless experience, linked smoothly to the other travel planning tools in the loop.

Corporate and Group Sales

Corporate and Group purchases need special tools and processes to meet the needs of travel departments, clubs, and specialized organizations. This can be a combination of special systems programming and human resources availability.

Purpose of Trip

Obviously, passengers have different requirements when traveling for business, leisure or VFR. The differences could relate to the air travel, but could also extend to rental cars, hotels, tours and so forth. Being able to move seamlessly between these modules is essential, and sometimes the same person will have different needs at different times based on their purpose of trip.

Self-Service versus Full Service

Airlines are increasingly developing facilities at the airport for passenger processing systems that give the passenger the "feeling" of being in touch with the reservations system directly. Such systems can be a time saver for the traveler as well as a cost saver for the airline. However, their functionality and degree of complexity must be carefully planned. Automated check-in devices are now beginning to include more than just getting boarding passes and baggage tags. The technology can be easily extended to changing flights, changing fare classes, getting upgrades and changing seats. These additional features add complexity and may make line-ups longer and increase frustration for those with simple requirements who only want to move quickly through the airport. It raises the question as to which functionalities should better be left in the hands of customer service agents. Is it easy or difficult and time-consuming to get refunds, change itineraries, replace a lost ticket, and arrange for special services such as handling pets or packaging skis or golf clubs? Again, what are the tradeoffs of complexity vs. simplicity?

Financial Protection and Insurance

The recent bankruptcy of Jetsgo in Canada is a perfect example of how a low-cost carrier can destroy the travel plans of thousands whilst taking their money as well. Certain people were protected from financial loss, but others were not. Passengers buying tickets using certain credit cards automatically had travel insurance and the same situation applied to those who used travel agents. However, the airline was still accepting reservations on its own website up to one hour before shutting down operations and those customers lost their money with no recourse. The travel industry in Canada is now considering a special indemnity fund to protect all travelers from such an occurrence, to put air travel on the same footing as buying other goods which customers can return and get their money back. The protection also needs to extend to purchases made via the web.

Inventory Control

It is not clear to passengers what access they have to the seat inventory. In other words, are some channels of distribution prevented from access to certain fare classes and the last available seat? These rules need to be transparent to the passenger.

Choice of Channels

Passengers feel that they cannot move easily and seamlessly between different channels, and get the right price and service levels from that channel in a consistent and repeatable fashion. If they want to use the web one day and then talk to a travel agent the next day, and then call the airline reservations center on a third occasion, will they see consistency in their treatment where appropriate, such as with regard to seat selection, upgrades, and so forth. The answer is a clear no. Passengers feel that they do not even get the same answer when they communicate with the same channel—call centers—let alone when communicating among different channels. Seasoned travelers are often heard recommending less frequent travelers to "wait a few minutes and call again" to get a different answer. Consequently, will passengers' travel experience be enhanced by the increasing number of channel choices available or will they only become more frustrated?

The Evolving Relationship with Agencies

Conventional airlines, under increasing pressure from passengers and unconventional airlines, have already made substantial progress in reducing their distribution costs. In the US, for example, the decline has been from about 20 percent of the total costs down to, in some cases, 8 percent. See Figure 6.1 The "Res & Other" category shown in Figure 6.1 refers to support services provided to the passenger. For example, in the 1995 time frame, a passenger might have made a reservation through one of the traditional channels and then called the airline's call center to ask for a seat assignment or had some other questions. These calls generated costs not only relating to the costs of agents answering calls but also the associated overhead in supporting such services. In the 2005 framework the category contains some of the same support costs as in 1995 but also the costs of reservations coming directly to the airline's website.

The largest component of the cost reduction is related to the reduction in agent commissions and overrides. With the elimination

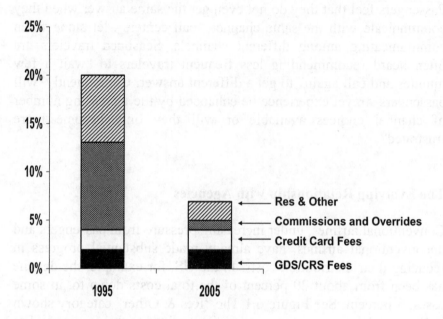

**Figure 6.1   Total Distribution Costs (North America) as a
Percentage of Revenue for a Typical US
Conventional Major Airline**

of base commissions and the introduction of e-tickets, the number of
offline US travel agents shrunk by more than one third, from about
33,700 in 1996 to about 20,900 in 2004. The numbers represent
estimates based on information obtained from various sources,
including the Airline Reporting Corporation. While many smaller
agencies have disappeared, consolidation has been rampant among
larger agencies, topped with the American Express' link up with
Rosenbluth. Because of this consolidation, large agencies still have
some leverage with airlines, which was substantiated recently when a
traditional GDS reportedly virtually shut down a major airline when
the airline wanted to pass on GDS fees to consumers.[5] As one analyst
noted, the GDS was able to have an enormous influence on the

airline by refusing to sell business class tickets in international markets.[6]

It is difficult to envision reducing commissions and overrides much more. Although consumers purchase online in growing numbers, conventional airlines are still heavily dependent on offline agents (who, in turn, are dependant on traditional GDSs, at least in the near term) for more than 50 percent of their revenues. It is well above that in some regions such as the Middle East. Moreover, airlines admit that this channel of distribution provides higher yields than the online channels. On the average a fare purchased online could be $50-100 lower than the average purchased through an offline channel.[7] This difference in fares could be accounted by the fact that a real person selling through an offline channel could persuade the passenger to purchase a higher value ticket by presenting such arguments as refundability. The ability to upsell clearly has value to airlines, and for agents it is a skill travel websites are unable to mimic.

Offline agents are changing their business model to show not only that they can bring in passengers that an airline does not have access to but also customers with a higher value. While it is true that agents bring in higher value bookings, part of that information is skewed in that the low fare passengers have abandoned travel agents. What agents now have is the higher corporate business. Therefore, if the $250 passenger is gone what is left is the $350 passenger? Although airlines are interested in their web sales, it is doubtful that an airline in the US can expect to get by that channel the potential passenger in Belfast or Kuala Lumpur with a complex itinerary. Here the agencies clearly add value.

Airlines have already started the process of examining the viability of developing their own relationships with agents. Even though the commissions have disappeared, some airlines question the need for the GDSs to be the financial go-between the airline and the agent. Airlines are considering going to agents directly. According to some, there is some value for an airline to decide what kind of a relationship it wants with a particular agent, depending on the size of the agency and the technology used. Some agencies have begun discussing whether they, and not the airline, would pay the GDS segment fees and pass these costs directly onto the passenger. While this model would benefit the airlines, it remains to be seen whether consumers would accept yet another fee added to their ticket prices.

The Growing Focus on Distribution Costs

As shown in Figure 6.1, the reduction in GDS fees has been fairly insignificant relative to the reduction in agent commissions and overrides. This is now the area of focus. Airlines have tried exchanging content for lower GDS fees, but they have seen mixed success in this initiative. While this strategy achieved lower GDS fees for airlines, it also enabled business travelers and some leisure travelers to have increased access to the fares in the lowest fare classes. The question, then, is whether the net impact of a significant dilution in yield is worth a reduction in the GDS costs? It is reasonable to assume that distribution costs could be reduced by another couple of percentage points by reducing or changing, not eliminating, the role of the intermediaries. Specific strategies for reducing distribution costs thus far have included:

- Increasing sales through an airline's own website through the promotion of low fares—including the introduction of best-fare guarantees as well as simpler fare structures.

- Reducing the traditional type of agent commissions even further in regions where they still exist and by introducing new financial incentives.

- Connecting directly to large corporate buyers and agents.

- Controlling access to the content—for example, making selected products and fares available or unavailable.

- Increasing the use of e-tickets.

- Finding new ways to not just reduce GDS costs but to reduce the dependence on traditional GDSs.

- Encouraging the use of emerging web-based, low-cost GDSs.

- Differentiating and optimizing within the different channel options.

- Introducing simpler and more rational pricing systems—both for customers and for agents.

- Exploring different ways to capitalize on the strength and resources of alliance partners.

Once distribution costs are in the 5-6 percent region, they are then approaching the level of distribution costs of unconventional airlines with distribution costs in the 3-6 percent bracket. However, the pressure on airlines to reduce distribution costs will continue in the foreseeable future as fares start to come down in intercontinental markets, particularly the fares for the premium cabins. See the discussion in the previous chapter.

Figure 6.2 shows the current general framework of the distribution chain. There are small differences among airlines but the key issue relating to the current framework is that airlines would prefer to deal directly with the passenger because cutting out the middleman (typically the GDS) results in lower costs. Unfortunately, for the airlines, cost cutting is not that simple. The problem relates to the money trail. Agencies receive payments from GDSs and from the airlines directly. Consequently, agencies may actually prefer to work with a GDS because of the fees they receive. An online agency, for example, may prefer to deal with a GDS who may be willing to pay a higher fee than the airline may be willing to pay to the agency. The airline, on the other hand, may decide to put pressure on the online agency by holding back some content. The next generation of GDSs is tempting to airlines because agency incentives are eliminated. GDS segment fees are reduced, and, since an agency is not receiving GDS payments, the airline can build a deeper relationship with the agency without GDS involvement. Therefore, it is imperative that airlines begin a dialogue with their major agency partners to discuss the shift to new generation GDS platforms. Given the right compensation structure, agencies will be willing to work with airlines to begin changing the distribution structure.

At the present time, large conventional US airlines achieve only 15-20 percent of their revenue through their websites and are spending between $100-250 million in GDS fees, depending on the size and network of the airline. This large expenditure explains the industry's relentless pursuit of reducing GDS fees through a variety of sources. They include alternative web-based GDSs that may be not only cheaper but claim that they can be more effective in enabling airlines to customize the distribution of their products and services.

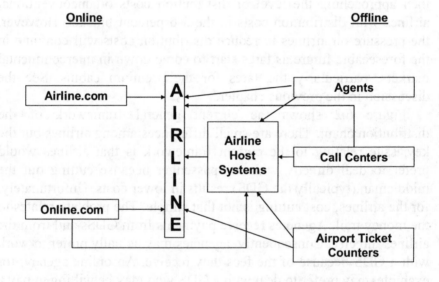

Figure 6.2 Current Relationship in the Distribution Chain

Given the interest of all airlines to go direct, there are a number of questions that must be addressed. Figure 6.3 summarizes the main issues and challenges regarding potential scenarios of the distribution chain. For example, from the supplier side, the critical issues relate to customers, employees and flexibility of the business model. While customers want choice, airlines need to get closer to the customer and as such need the capability to gather customer intelligence.

Airlines would also like to have systems that increase the productivity of staff by getting the most value out of customer engagement—from enhancing customer satisfaction to reducing customer contact time to enhancing revenue from incremental sales. Finally, airlines want flexibility, given the uncertainties relating to the emerging business models of agents and GDSs. On the technical side the issues range from supplier links to distribution control.

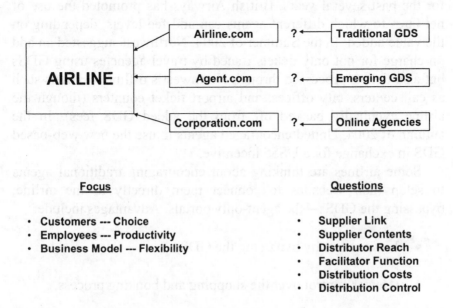

Focus

- Customers --- Choice
- Employees --- Productivity
- Business Model --- Flexibility

Questions

- Supplier Link
- Supplier Contents
- Distributor Reach
- Facilitator Function
- Distribution Costs
- Distribution Control

Figure 6.3 Future Relationship in the Distribution Chain

Conventional airlines have not yet reached a critical mass in their direct distribution channel to have leverage with the GDSs and the agents. Conventional airlines need to reach 50 percent of the sales through their websites before they will be able to exercise much more power. On the other hand, conventional airlines cannot ignore the GDSs if they want to sell their products in regions where they have limited presence. Therefore, the solution relates to finding the business model that aligns costs and benefits among airlines, GDSs, agents and passengers. There is, however, a need to push down costs. For example, the use of numerous search engines may add significant volume (but not increased passengers) to an airline's systems, leading to an increase in costs. Consequently distribution costs need to be examined well beyond the level of transaction fees. Furthermore the cost-benefit alignment needs to be flexible to adapt to the fast-changing environment.

Airlines have already started examining their pricing systems to align them with the changing landscape of distribution. For example, for the past several years, British Airways has promoted the use of net fares to which different agents can add fee levels, depending on the value added. In the Summer of 2004, Northwest suggested an add on charge for not only tickets issued by travel agencies using GDSs but also tickets processed through Northwest's offline locations such as call centers, city offices, and airport ticket counters (though the airline eventually backed off from the added GDS fees). In the autumn of 2004, United encouraged agents to use the new web-based GDS in exchange for a US$5 incentive.

Some airlines are thinking about encouraging traditional agents to setup their websites to connect them directly to the airline, bypassing the GDSs—the agent-only portals. Advantages include:[8]

- Lower costs by bypassing the GDSs.

- Greater control over the shopping and booking process.

- Flexibility in the airline-agent financial arrangement.

- Customized service from the airline (e.g., upgrades).

- Closing access to competitive data from the Marketing Information Data Tapes (MIDT).

Optimizing Airline Distribution Costs

The changing landscape in distribution is providing airlines opportunities to take advantage of diversity and optimize based on such considerations as revenues, costs, control, functionality, reach, content and communications. Here are some examples:

- As to revenue, airlines can take advantage of opportunities provided by deregulation of GDSs. For example, they can pay higher fees to a GDS if the GDS can provide a disproportionately higher market share. It was partly this aspect that led to the introduction of regulation in the first place. This strategy can now perhaps provide the most value in an airline's non-hub markets. Conversely, a reduction in commission fees and transaction fees could be offset by higher forms of GDS fees for shifting market shares. However, if the higher fees received by GDSs are shared by the GDS with the agents, then we are back to square one.

- As to costs, the issue is not just direct costs of the distribution channel but also the indirect costs. The channel selection criteria need to include, for example, the impact on revenue accounting and revenue management, since there are significant costs involved in publishing fares and reconciling fares.

- As to control, one issue relates to how an airline's seats are distributed. An airline's concern for control lies at least in three areas: (1) the level of fees, (2) inventory and display, and (3) technical aspects such as re-ticketing and monitoring of time restrictions.

- As to communications, the issue relates to how an airline can communicate, for example, a lower fare that might be available to some passengers through some channels but not to others?

Consequently, given the (a) limited access to global markets even for large global carriers, (b) control by, at least the mega traditional offline travel agencies of the corporate market, and (c) the large investments required to bring the business directly to the airline, one can see a need for a re-examination by the conventional airlines of their distribution strategies to optimize on the available diversity resulting from the different price-service options offered by different channels.

In summary, while conventional airlines are lowering their distribution costs, building brands, making it easier for customers to do business with them and segmenting the marketplace (instead of being all things to all people), there is a need to pick up the pace and integrate the distribution decision more carefully with decisions on other elements of the marketing mix. The most important requirement, however, continues to be related to gaining a better understanding of consumer behavior.

Conclusions

Aside from the need to reduce and control costs, three major forces—changes in consumer behavior, expansion of technology, and marketplace deregulation—are having an enormous impact on the business model of the three major members in the airline distribution chain—airlines, agents and GDSs. While the ultimate business models of all members within the distribution chain will be heavily oriented toward the customer, the situation in the near term is likely to be muddy. For example, while passengers want simplicity and clarity, they are likely to experience complexity and confusion as agents and GDSs consolidate and as airlines introduce fundamental changes in their fare structures. And as airlines examine alternative business models within the area of distribution, the top consideration must be the passenger—not only the value that the airline provides to the passenger but also the value of the passenger to the airline. Consequently distribution strategies need to take into account not only such considerations as cost of the distribution channel but also the value of the channel relating to such aspects as revenue and accumulation of customer intelligence. Just as airlines will look at passengers differently so will agents by changing from being order takers to order makers. Passengers want either more service for the same price or they want a lower price for the same service. Passengers want to shop and they want the members of the distribution chain to provide choices, offer them some control, and generate credibility and trust in the product.

Notes

[1]   Agents are divided into two categories. "Offline agents" refers to traditional brick and mortar agents. "Online agents" refers to agencies, such as Expedia, distributing the travel related products through their websites. The term "facilitators" refers to providers of technology and services for agents to display the content and make reservations for customers. GDSs (global distribution systems) refer to the traditional systems such as Amadeus, Galileo, Sabre and Worldspan. The term "web-based GDSs" refers to the new generation of web-based GDSs that use the web to store, search, and retrieve information instead of mainframes. Examples include the systems being developed and marketed by ITA Software and G2 Switchworks.

[2]   Meta-search refers to the use of travel websites that pull results from multiple websites.

[3]   Field, David and Mark Pilling, "The last legacy", *Airline Business*, March 2005, pp. 48-51.

[4]   According to the recently formed Coalition for Fair Access to Reservations in Europe, deregulation within Europe could take place at a slower pace. See *Travel Distribution Report*, 30 May 2005, Volume 13, Number 12, p. 95.

[5]   *Travel Distribution Report*, 18 October 2004, Volume 12, Number 21, p. 165.

[6]   Blank, Jared, analyst for the *Online Travel Review*, *Travel Distribution Report*, 18 October 2004, Volume 12, Number 21, p. 165.

[7]   McKinsey Quarterly Article, December 2004.

[8]   *Travel Distribution Report*, Vol. 13, No. 4, January 31, 2005, pp. 27-28.

Chapter 7

Developing Truly Integrated Alliances

In one form or another, airline alliances have existed for years—interlining in the early years, joint maintenance in the late 1960s and joint marketing since the late 1980s. Currently, strategic alliances represent a major force in the global airline industry. Initially set up to overcome the restrictive nature of bilateral agreements, they began to be marketed as a way of providing a seamless experience to the global traveler and at the same time increasing value for the shareholders of member airlines. Unfortunately, despite their stated and partially implemented customer and share holder orientation, they have neither achieved high levels of customer satisfaction nor the full potential benefits of joint operations.

One explanation is the imbalance between the high expectations built up by alliances and the low performance delivered by them. The explanation for this imbalance is due to numerous factors such as differences in culture, mistrust among the partners, each partner's desire to maintain flexibility and the impact of alliance governance structures on the group dynamics and the decision making process. To put it simply, members think of alliances more like "dating" and less like the old fashioned "marriage". Since the relationship is not forever, companies do not make commitments and investments as they have an eye to the exit costs and are wary of investing in IT systems and consolidation of properties. This chapter discusses customer perceptions and some considerations for the successful implementation of alliances. The chapter ends with an example, from outside the airline industry, of a successful alliance from the viewpoint of customers worldwide—VISA International.

Recognizing Customer Perceptions

Some customers feel that alliances do not produce the consistent, efficient and seamless travel experience as proclaimed and communicated by airlines. The lack of consistent service is a major problem faced by individual airlines worldwide. Within an alliance the complexity of this problem grows exponentially. In certain areas, alliance partners have tried to standardize services and have succeeded. In others, they have had a lot less success, either because of unresolved implementation issues among the members themselves or because members had little or no control in the areas under the jurisdiction of airports and governments.

Although researchers have analyzed customer perceptions of failures, shortcomings and recoveries relating to products and services for years, most of the research was limited to products and services provided by individual companies. Recently, researchers have begun to examine customers' impressions of products and services offered by alliances. One insightful example is the pragmatic research conducted through interviews in Hong Kong.[1] The results provide some insightful information about alliances from customers' perspectives.

Based on a broad spectrum of input, customers' perception of alliances can be categorized in the following three areas: consistency, communication and brand and options.

Consistency Issues

- The uniformity across the products offered by carriers within the alliance is lot less than passengers are led to believe, and the product disparities that exist within airline alliances hamper efforts to build a strong and consistent alliance brand. The results of one research study show, for example, that through its alliance (Qualiflyer), Swissair diluted its valuable brand by predominantly selecting lower quality airlines as members.[2] Part of the problem is understandable. Alliances invest in marketing programs to distinguish themselves and are constantly seeking ways to differentiate themselves in the eyes of their customers. A traditional marketing precept in the airline industry is that airlines do not want to make their products uniform. That is the one thing that differentiates them. There is a wide difference among the business class products of different airlines—seat configuration, and product features such as the availability of electric power for laptop computers and Internet service. Premium passengers used to flying most of their trips in the premium cabin of their base airline (with a 2x2 configuration and a lie-flat bed in business class) will be surprised and disappointed by the premium cabin of a partner where they may be assigned a "middle seat" (that reclines less than 160 degrees and is less comfortable) in the partner's so-called comparable business class.

- Although the aim of successful alliances should be to make customer travel between any two points completely seamless, the reality is that some alliances have failed to even provide sufficient training for members' employees to answer routine customer questions. There are cases where one partner's employees cannot correctly explain to passengers the airport procedures on flights operating to or from an alliance partner's foreign hub. For example, all alliance employees should be able to tell a passenger whether the passenger will be required to clear customs and immigrations at a hub airport before proceeding to a connecting flight, even though the ultimate airport is also an international airport. The answer varies from country to country. In the US, a passenger flying from London into New York and connecting to Cincinnati does need to clear immigration and customs in New York. In India, a passenger flying from London to Mumbai and connecting to Cochin does not need to clear immigration and customs in Mumbai. Partners within the same alliance sometimes do not know the answers and, worse, some agents have provided wrong answers leading to situations where passengers have missed their connections.

- Some top tier status members in frequent flyer programs do not feel that they get the same recognition from their airline's partners in the strategic alliances. If an airline wants loyalty from its top passengers, then it better ensure that the elite status members are recognized consistently throughout the systems of all alliance partners, and at every passenger touch point.

Communication and Brand Issues

- According to some passengers, there is a large gap between the messages communicated about the value of the alliance for passengers and the products/services delivered. Passengers are told about the benefits of alliances in commercial advertisements in the media, in signs at airports, in in-flight magazines and in inserts contained with mileage statements. The performance does not consistently match the expectations.

- It is difficult for passengers to get adequate information from one airline let alone get information from a strategic alliance partner. Just think about finding out information (the location and the appropriate partner) about a delayed flight or what would happen to passengers who miss a connection. Just imagine the problems faced by a passenger traveling on a ticket issued by one airline checking in for an overbooked flight of an alliance partner?[3]

- Although individual airlines themselves are reasonably well known brand names, airline alliances have not succeeded in building well known brands at levels recognized in other industries. The problem is one of consistency that has prevented airline alliances from producing a brand synergy like some other businesses have achieved. Companies like VISA and MasterCard invest to become global brands. As discussed below, for example, VISA sponsors the Olympics.

Similarly, MasterCard is the official sponsor of the 2006 World Cup.

- Although not an issue with respect to the large, well known global airlines, some passengers have concerns regarding the safety and security of lesser known airline members of the alliance.

- The brand images of some flag carriers are tied very closely to their home countries. If a member airline's brand equity is strong then the airline risks it in being compromised under a weaker brand umbrella.

Option Issues

- From some passengers' perspectives, network integration coupled with code share tactics meant a "harmonization" of schedules, resulting in fewer options for travel.

- Similarly, from some customers' perspective, there are fewer price options in situations in which competition is "organized". Yet, research shows that three forms of cooperation (alliance membership, code sharing and antitrust immunity) have led to a 27 percent reduction in interline fares.[4]

- There are passengers who feel that they have ended up traveling on airlines (due to code shares) that they wanted to avoid.

- Finally, in recent years there has been activity relating to consolidation within alliances. For example, Air France was in one alliance and KLM was in a different alliance. However, the Air France-KLM consolidation led to discussions regarding the consolidation between alliances. Some researchers are exploring the following question. While airlines have benefited from higher profits, do merger and alliance consolidations harm consumers?[5]

The main point is that airline alliances have only partially succeeded in providing to passengers all of the communicated benefits in the areas of product and brand consistency. Even worse, is perhaps the gap between the airlines' perception that passengers get more options and passengers who feel that they get fewer options.

Balancing Alliance Benefits

The pace of globalization was stimulated in the 1970s and 1980s by an increase in economic integration and technology. While most industries were able to take advantage by being able to participate in international markets and increasing their international trade (through a variety of strategies, including mergers and acquisitions), the airline industry remained an exception due to the existence of restrictive bilateral agreements as well as ownership and control rules. Consequently, the airline industry turned to alliances as a way of participating in the globalization of markets.[6] Some researchers call this the second best solution to achieve free trade in world aviation.[7] Some airline executives call this development, "an artificial solution to an artificial problem". Nevertheless, alliances provided not only a way of entering some international markets, they also provided a way for airlines to lessen the impact of uncertainty and instability associated with global economies.[8] As a result of joining alliances, airlines have reported some revenue benefits of expanded global networks via code sharing. The best solution for true participation in the globalization of businesses is worldwide open skies—market access, mergers and acquisitions and subsidies, with no government interference. However, it is difficult to envision such a scenario in the near term due to the risk of large scale bankruptcies, loss of national airlines and the dominance of a few large alliances around a few large airlines.

Alliances have also provided some benefits for passengers. Some international passengers have been better served due to greater, albeit, not yet seamless, coordination of services. However, the benefits, for both airlines and passengers, are far from reaching their full potential. The reason may be due to the fact that (a) most airline alliances seem to be more operationally focused than customer focused, and (b) for a broad spectrum of reasons (some discussed below), alliance partners are, in some cases, not willing to and, in other cases, not able to exploit all synergies on the cost side (joint in-sourcing and out-sourcing of flight operations, for example). The following section summarizes the actual and potential benefits on both sides.

Airline Benefits

- Some industries, the airline industry included, have some unique economic characteristics: Profit is a very small number and it is the difference between two very large numbers, large revenues but equally large costs. Fixed costs are high. Consequently, on some flights just a couple of passengers can make the difference between profit and loss. Alliances have provided their members a few extra passengers per flight. Moreover, airlines have used the incremental passengers obtained through alliances to take advantage of the economies of density (lower unit costs of larger aircraft) and economies of scope (lower unit costs with an increase in the number of products offered).

- The current hypercompetitive environment has enabled alliance members to reduce some costs and increase revenues. Costs have been saved by (a) not serving some markets and having the alliance partner do it, and (b) eliminating the ground handling, airport passenger services, and sales infrastructure and using the partner's facilities—particularly beneficial initiatives for international operations. However, costs have not been reduced to the level possible for two reasons. First, each member wants to "game the deal" to its own advantage. Second, operationally, alliances add complexity and complexity adds to costs. Revenue has been increased by having access to new markets without actually serving these markets as well as by capitalizing on the local knowledge of partners of the idiosyncrasies of local markets. As in the case of costs, the true benefits on the revenue side are limited. The incremental passengers are not all incremental through stimulation of the market. Rather, most incremental passengers are diversions from other alliances. Therefore, these initiatives have enabled, although to a limited degree, member airlines to improve their international competitiveness by enhanced (a) market presence and global reach, as well as (b) resource utilization.

- Many airlines have joined alliances for purely defensive reasons. Having seen competitors form alliances, some airlines have felt compelled to join an alliance to protect their traffic which is likely to be drawn away by the competitive alliances. Moreover, an airline that did not join could be facing a reduction in its interlining capability. It is this defensive motivation that led airlines to ask not whether to join but which alliance to join. On the other side, one alliance can also preempt another alliance getting a particular airline to join that group.

- It is also a way of reducing competition, enabling one partner to reduce capacity without losing market share or access to traffic. It not only reduces competition with the partner but strengthens it against the third competitor in the marketplace. However, the reduction in competition only results in benefits if yields can be raised.

- New technology is expensive (for example, ultra long haul aircraft) and it could be shared. If, for example, an airline such as United had only a limited number of routes for a specialized aircraft, it could coordinate its schedules with its partners such as Singapore and Thai Airways.

- It is also a way to conduct business in this uncertain global business environment. Alliances provide some opportunities to enter new markets without a substantial investment, thereby enabling an airline to determine if the market can be developed enough to warrant additional services and achieve a reasonable margin..

- Alliances can provide access for a weaker partner to some knowledge or expertise of the stronger partner. Examples include expertise in such areas as revenue management, cargo handling, and knowledge relating, for instance, to the travel purchasing behavior of corporations that are based in the area. However, access to such knowledge can work both ways in that one partner may get hold of some critical piece of information that may have a high competitive value for the other partner.

Passenger Benefits

The increasing globalization of businesses has increased the need for passengers to travel all over the world, creating a need not only for a global network (scope benefits of network coverage and frequency) but also access to restricted but highly desirable airports, London's Heathrow and Tokyo's Narita being high on the list. Second, passengers want seamless travel and high frequencies. Third, passengers want more extensive loyalty programs—ability to vacation in exotic places. Seamless travel so far has resulted in minor improvements in intra-alliance interlining. There is still no real seamless travel: inconsistencies abound when it comes to e-ticketing, airline changes on short notice, cabin class standards, call center assistance and frequent flyer profile sharing.

Although both airlines and customers have had some positive results from alliances from their own perspective, the compelling advantages for both the traveling public and the shareholders are yet to be developed. An alliance could be successful if it was designed, first, around passengers' needs, and, second, around the shareholders of member airlines. From the passengers' perspective it would add value if the design was to provide new service to stimulate travel rather than simply diverting passengers from one alliance to another. Most of the time alliances have not really created new passengers. They have simply diverted them. Occasionally, however, they have created new demand or at least stimulated demand. The nonstop service between Amsterdam and Memphis is a case in point. Without the alliance this service would not exist. Similarly, from shareholders' viewpoint the value of the alliance would increase substantially if the partners had antitrust immunity. However, in the airline industry, it appears that (a) each member's interests come first, (b) operational concerns come second, and (c) genuine passengers' concerns come third. Consequently, there may be some value in exploring the cost effectiveness of consortia. See the discussion below.

Implementing Successful Alliances

The premise of this book is that airlines should build value through passenger analysis, passenger insights and customer engagement. What seams obvious is to select the strategic segments, get some meaningful insights into these segments and then build the business designs around these valued customers. If most airlines have had trouble doing this around their own passengers, the problem becomes much more complex for performing these tasks around passengers brought in by partners (one of the objectives for partners in an alliance). As pointed out in Chapters 1 and 8, airlines have had difficulty in figuring out the ins and outs of customer engagement with their own customers, let alone with the customers of alliance partners. If managing customer relations at various touch points is a real challenge for one airline, think about this challenge within the context of an alliance. Let us consider some specific hurdles before discussing some strategies for successfully implementing alliances.

The biggest hurdle is perhaps the huge difference in member airline business objectives. Each airline is concerned with its own financial results and will want initiatives that provide it the benefits it needs. Alliances require compromises and some members are not willing to accept compromises. Examples include adopting common standards such as common IT platforms (for reservation and departure control) and access to passenger data bases (for upgrades criteria and consistent recognition). In the case of the latter, for example, for competitive reasons, some partners are not willing to exchange such data bases.

The achievement of genuine and significant reductions in costs requires rationalization of networks. Unfortunately, for reasons of egos and national pride, a number of small airlines are not willing to become feeders to the relevant partners. Some members feel that benefits are unbalanced. For example, one partner may fly the high yield flights (first flight in the morning short haul business market or the long haul portion of a connecting flight) and the other partner flies the low yield flights (the flight in the mid afternoon or the flight to the leisure destinations). Finally, some small carriers have a problem with the costs of joining the alliance (up-front fees as well as the costs of converting, for example, their IT systems into alliance-compatible systems). They also are concerned about the costs involved if a partner wants to leave, including the opportunity costs of re-establishment in case of a breakup.

Before discussing various aspects of successful alliance implementation, it is first necessary to discuss a number of issues relating to membership in an alliance. The following are just a few sequential questions:

- Should an airline even join an alliance? Can an airline operate successfully outside of a multilateral alliance and work instead with a portfolio of bilateral alliances? Emirates, Japan Airlines and Virgin Atlantic do. Most airlines, obviously not all, have felt the need to join simply because almost all others have joined. This is especially true for airlines that depend on connecting traffic or lack access to premium fare traffic outside their home markets. South African Airways, for example, held out but then changed its mind to access the premium traffic, particularly out of the UK. There are even more complicated issues relating to alliance membership. How does an airline establish a relationship with another airline that is outside the alliance partnership? For example, Qantas and Air New Zealand are in two different multilateral alliances. Should Qantas and Air New Zealand also be able to align themselves? In the case of Singapore Airlines, it is in one multilateral alliance but also has a substantial equity in Virgin Atlantic, an airline not within a multilateral alliance. What are the ramifications of this arrangement? Finally, there is the issue of national and strategic importance of networks for economic and political development.

- If multilateral, which one of the global alliances should the airline join and what is the context of the membership (for example, equity, sharing of codes, frequent flyer programs, airport lounges, maintenance, flight operations and so forth)? Regarding the first point, the selection of the alliance involves some tough questions such as the degree of network overlap. For example, Thai and Singapore Airlines are in the same alliance but have significant overlap within their networks. The second point also has some tough questions. For example, what would happen if the ownership and control rules are changed? Then those airlines that became regional operators for major partners would have a hard time re-establishing themselves in the marketplace in terms of rebuilding fleet, brand, and so forth.

These very difficult questions and answers depend on numerous sets of additional questions relating, first, to the objective of the airline—growth, cost reductions, access to key markets, airports, or types of traffic (for example, China, Heathrow and high fare passengers). While the first set of questions refers to objectives, the second set may refer to equally important areas such as similarity or differences in culture, size, strategies, services and brand. Another set of questions may relate to the costs of joining and separating.

Based on the aforementioned concerns for mutual benefits for passengers and member airlines, Figure 7.1 shows examples of six areas relating to critical success factors. Given that the product and service consistency aspects have already been discussed, let us move to the other five areas.

Cultural Harmony

Cultural harmony transcends many areas such as: trust, openness, respect, and transparency among partners; and power plays over control, jurisdiction, governance and decision making processes. It also touches the willingness to make compromises (relating to brands, GDSs, reservation criteria and pricing policies) to capitalize on synergy to create and build relationships. Moreover, it is needed to persuade front-line employees to overcome their strong emotional ties to their own airlines to promote the alliance. The real issue relates to balancing the need for independence and interdependence?[9]

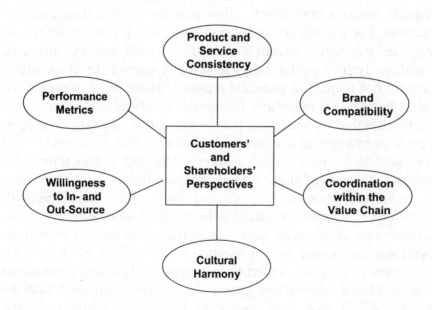

Figure 7.1 Examples of Alliance Key Success Factors

Performance Metrics

Meaningful performance metrics must be developed that go beyond the standard count of routes, passengers, or airports and the placement of each of these measures against competition. Measurements are needed for an airline to understand the value of its contribution (say the value of each partner's hub on each side of the Atlantic) to such critical areas as (a) the balance of benefits, and (b) the cost effectiveness for a minor partner on a given route to let the major partners offer the service. On the latter point, as a case in point, British Midland is a minor player across the Atlantic. Would it be more cost effective for United to take over the services provided by British Midland?

Willingness to In- and Out-Source

The real benefits come from partners sharing profit or revenue which requires antitrust immunity to allow partners to align their financial interests. For sharing assets (aircraft and crews), there is no reason why an expensive aircraft's utilization could not be increased significantly by keeping it flying virtually around the clock (other than for commercial or technical reasons). There are, however, three major hurdles: (a) regulatory (bilaterals, certifications—aircraft and crew), (b) labor contracts and provisions, and (c) management egos. One clear example of a management barrier is that most airlines will not agree to a common specification for aircraft and therefore will not get the benefit of either volume purchase (minor benefit), relative to cross utilization of aircraft and crews (the major benefit). Therefore, it appears that airlines have relied more heavily on the revenue side of alliances (access to traffic), than on cost reductions (with the real savings coming through higher utilization of common equipment and not just superficial savings through joint purchase of fuel or plastic spoons and forks). How many airlines would be willing to sell their long haul fleet and let the partners fly the prestigious high visibility routes, even if it will save a huge amount of money, not to mention a substantial reduction in complexity? Moreover, even when airlines do participate in joint procurement, in certain cases some members try to "squeeze" their own partners. One partner buying services from another partner looks at the buyer as a captive purchaser. Once again, there is a critical need to develop metrics to measure the performance of the alliance.[10] Just as there must be metrics to evaluate alliances from the partners' perspective, there must be equivalent metrics to measure the value of alliances from the customers' perspectives.

Brand Compatibility

From the perspective of the brand, the most critical issue relates to finding a balance between an airline marketing its own brand and at the same time marketing itself through the alliance brand. Should an airline allow its own brand to become subordinate to the alliance brand? Airlines say that they do work together. However, is there real trust? Take two examples. First, passengers have found it possible to get substantially lower fares from different partners for reservation on exactly the same flight. Second, one partner can advertise in another partner's home country its own flights to its own home country.

Coordination within the Value Chain

Coordination within the value chain provides mutual benefits not only for customers and shareholders but all members within the value chain, including employees. Jonathan Tisch, Chairman and CEO of Loews Hotels, provides a good example of how to succeed through partnerships with six groups: customers, employees, owners, other businesses, communities and governments. In his book, he makes a strong case for using the power of partnerships for "getting from me to we".[11] He also provides good examples of turning customers into partners, for example, by linking with customer communities. Success depends on (a) recognizing that organizations do not exist in vacuums, and (b) redefining the terms of traditional business relationships and transforming them from adversarial to cooperative. As for partnering with customers, examples of other companies that have connected with their customer communities include Harley Davidson and NASCAR. There are 800,000 members in the Harley Davidson Owners Group and there are 75 million people who call themselves NASCAR fans; 36 million are reported to have attended the car races in 2003.[12]

Starbucks provides another example of leveraging a truly integrated alliance, not only to create a hugely successful company, but to create a market niche in an industry where none existed. The success of Starbucks is very much dependent on its competency to develop truly integrated alliances with members in the value chain. Consider, just two members—suppliers and communities. When Starbucks negotiated a contact with its main supplier the Costco Wholesale Corporation (Costco), there were two key considerations. First, would there be brand issues given that Costco was a discounter and Starbucks was a provider of a premium coffee drinking experience for its customers. Second, instead of negotiating the lowest price from the supplier, the strategy changed to how the two companies can work to "satisfy their mutual customers" and enhance their mutual value. For details, see the case study by Larraine Segil.[13] As for alliance with communities, Starbucks works very closely with communities around the stores, at the country level and the global level, and the countries of origin of the coffee itself. With respect to the first group of communities, Starbucks has clearly developed partnerships with communities wherever Starbucks' customers may be found—airports, hotels, bookstores, and so forth.[14]

In the case of airlines, significant value can be derived from alliances with other members in the travel value chain. Recent research shows the value of airline-airport alliances with cooperation in three areas: capacity, marketing and security. One specific example of a capacity oriented alliance between an airline and an airport is reported to be between Lufthansa and the Munich Airport. Lufthansa participated financially in the construction of a terminal, reducing the financial obligations of the airport. In return, Lufthansa was able to have some input regarding the planning and use of the terminal, input that not only helps Lufthansa but also other members of the Star alliance, not to mention the ultimate customers.[15] However, just as the antitrust immunity can have a significant impact on the value of airline alliances, governments' competition policy can also have significant impact on the value of airline-airport alliances.

From experience, it is clear that alliance member airlines have found it particularly difficult to deal with these six critical factors. The difficulties relate to the limitations on governance and the desire to promote the self interest of individual carriers.[16] For instance, the real savings in costs result from sharing flight operations. Instead, due to a broad spectrum of reasons including those mentioned above as well as government and labor restrictions, the sharing of resources has been limited to code, check-in facilities, airport lounges and frequent flyer programs. As long as alliance members have an exit option in the back of their minds, they will not give up resources and competencies they consider necessary for "a life after the alliance".

In some ways, alliances could become history, especially if governments change ownership and control rules and allow mergers, acquisitions, and consolidations, as appears to be the case. That scenario leads to the conclusion that alliances could be superseded by consortia that are able to really manage true seamless value. Such a seamless travel experience requires the integrated management of the crucial passenger-facing functions:

- Network design—number and type of hubs and routes.

- Fleet and facilities—planning and acquisition.

- Pricing structure—for mass, corporate, and personal travel.

- Cabin configurations—number and type by market.

- Airport processes—differentiated by customer segment.

- Integration of ground services—car rentals, shuttle buses, hotel check-in.

Finally, there is one other scenario regarding alliances that is being explored. This scenario relates to unconventional airlines and it has two parts. First, what would be the feasibility and impact on current alliances if the unconventional airlines also formed their own alliances (for instance, an alliance among WestJet, jetBlue, and easyJet)? This question is being explored from many different angles: How would this happen? What would have to change? Are there any market factors that would facilitate or prevent such alliances from taking place? Could the code sharing experience between Southwest and ATA be the icebreaker? Second, what would be the feasibility and the impact on current alliances if some conventional airline members of the current alliances started to develop their own alliances with unconventional airlines (for instance, an alliance between jetBlue and American)? Let us not forget the successful experience of the alliance between Costco (the discounter brand) and Starbucks (the premium brand).

An Example of True Partnerships with a Real Brand: VISA International

In one form or another, airline alliances have existed for years, but to date no airline alliance has succeeded at promoting and delivering a global brand that is superior to the brands of the individual members. To build a respected global brand, an alliance must be entirely customer focused, and earn the trust of its customers by consistently delivering efficient, convenient, and seamless service where ever, and when ever, the customers encounter the brand. Airline alliances have not yet evolved to that level of passenger acceptance.

A customer focused global consortia that is very successful, and that provides synergies for members is VISA, the financial services company that consumers consistently rate as the best overall card. At the heart of VISA is a globally recognized brand that is more valuable than the individual brands of its many members. Built over the last 30 years by the efforts and investments of VISA and its members working in partnership, VISA now ranks among the world's top 10 most valuable brands, and leads the financial services category.[17]

The VISA brand has been positioned upon the promise of empowerment. Consumers, businesses and institutions have the opportunity to accomplish what is important to them. The brand's sterling reputation has been earned by promoting and delivering unsurpassed acceptance, reliability and convenience. No other payment brand, and few other brands anywhere, enjoy the level of recognition and appeal that VISA holds around the world.

But the VISA brand doesn't operate in isolation. It is a well orchestrated collaboration among an extremely diverse group of members. At the center of a global seamless payment system conducted between issuing banks, merchants, acquiring banks and cardholders, the VISA brand always works in alliance with others, essentially as a co-brand. Having established its worldwide reputation, the VISA brand now imparts and gains equities from its partnerships. The VISA brand is successful because it creates synergies from the benefits provided to individual members of the alliance. For merchants, the VISA brand provides access to and guaranteed payment from the widest possible customer base; handles financial transactions conveniently, efficiently, and reliably; and allows merchants to better meet customer needs by offering the ease of electronic payments, whether in traditional or e-commerce environments.

For its issuing members, customer recognition of the VISA brand adds to the value of the members' own brands, driving greater total revenue. It is the VISA brand more than the individual members' own brands that ensures that bank customers will enjoy unquestioned global acceptance and reliability, and innovation in payment. The bottom line is the trust VISA has created and nurtured among its varied partners. This trust is the most valuable brand asset VISA seeks to guard, protect and enhance at every opportunity.

As an industry leader with 60-plus percent global market share in the payments industry, VISA is constantly working to ensure its continued relevance in an ever-changing marketplace.[18] Over the years, VISA has established alliances with the world's most respected and celebrated brands, spanning many business, sports and entertainment sectors. This includes prominent partnerships with the Olympics, NFL, Disney, Marriott, McDonalds, Sony, Le Meridien, British Airways and many others.

Besides the business elements of the relationships, VISA closely examines the attributes and brand equity any partnership will deliver. This is key if VISA is to create the valued marketing platforms its member banks utilize for their programs and their customers. This creates a virtuous circle of investment in co-branded activities and promotions that drive sales of VISA products and services before and during the events.

VISA's brand promise also involves continuous innovation so that users enjoy unprecedented ease and security. One example of VISA's commitment to innovation is the recent advancements in smart card technology, integrating an intelligent chip that stores more than 100 times the information contained on a traditional magnetic stripe card. The chip allows the addition of multiple functions on top of a VISA credit or debit payment, such as transit passes and loyalty cards, all in a single card. Chip technology is central to VISA's vision of universal commerce, a world where buyers and sellers can use VISA to pay for anything, anywhere, at any time, using any device.

In order to stay current with the latest developments in emerging technologies, VISA forms and invests in strategic alliances with both current and emerging technology companies. In working with these partners, VISA helps define and shape the future of electronic payments, including the standards, security and systems. As an example, VISA is working with Royal Philips to explore opportunities in proximity technologies—the ability to conduct payment or information transactions wirelessly through smart cards or any number of other devices such as cell phones and PDAs. VISA also formed a strategic alliance with Tripwire to develop and deploy products and services designed to help VISA improve security against data or network integrity breaches.

As Internet commerce continues to grow, VISA is also looking into ways to improve security, including an alliance with Arcot, which has been a key in the development of the Verified by VISA program. The program is designed to reduce the potential for Internet fraud and increase consumer confidence when shopping online. With VISA's overall fraud rate half of what it was six years ago, Verified by VISA is expected to reduce Internet transaction disputes by at least 50 percent.

VISA has proven itself a truly extendable brand, validating its strength and ability to move into the future. Recent examples include expanding the debit and prepaid product platforms that have created more efficient payment options for transportation, health care and various government services. Identification and authorization innovations include online use of the brand with Verified by VISA. Other "new ways to pay" include mobile telephony "top up" capabilities, chip and contact-less technology.

VISA has become one of the strongest, most widely known and trusted brands around the world because of its ability to successfully create alliances with others. The electronic payments sector is likely to remain a robust, growth oriented opportunity for the foreseeable future and VISA is a brand positioned as the preferred partner to realize that future.

VISA's experience provides significant insights for the airline industry.

- VISA focuses on innovation as a brand promise for a simple reason—without new technologies and services, it will continue to face pressures on margins. Unlike 30 years ago when simply creating the VISA payments system was innovation, today the organization faces increased competition, regulation and economic pressures. While 99.99 percent systems reliability is phenomenal, it is also expected. It will protect its business and future growth.

- The airline sector should recognize that it has also become more commoditized over the past 10 years. While there will always be some high-end and experiential travel, this will be less and less the norm. Travel has become common. Once a service becomes a utility, differentiation is extremely difficult. To have phone service used to be special. It is now nearly universal. Dial tone is expected and not particularly appreciated.

- The discount airlines are trying to create many "flavors" of discounted experiences, so there will appear to be innovative new concepts. Most, however, will be short-lived because true differentiation will only occur around new offerings that impact margins.

Conclusions

Under the current circumstances, most airlines will continue to participate in alliances, given their cost effectiveness as well as the possible impact of non participation. However, the true success of an alliance can only be measured from two perspectives—the customers and the shareholders. From the viewpoint of the customers, a successful alliance must (a) develop a unique selling proposition perception, (b) deliver superior interline experience, and (c) maintain a reliable product profile over all classes. From the shareholders' perspective, the alliance must (a) exploit all synergies on the cost side (joint sourcing, joint backup services), and (b) build a network of synergistic specialized carriers.

Notes

[1]   Weber, Karin and Beverly Sparks, "Consumer attributions and behavioral responses to service failures in strategic airline alliance settings", *Journal of Air Transport Management*, Volume 10 (2004), pp. 361-367. This particular research was conducted by analyzing the results of an in-depth survey of 22 carefully selected frequent flyers. The interviews took place in Hong Kong and each interview averaged 45 minutes.

[2]   Knorr, Andreas and Andreas Arndt, "Alliance strategy and the fall of Swissair: a comment", *Journal of Air Transport Management*, Volume 10 (2004), p. 122.

[3]   Weber, Karin and Beverley Sparks, "Consumer attributions and behavioral responses to service failures in strategic airline alliance settings", *Journal of Air Transport Management*, Volume 10 (2004), p. 364.

4   Brueckner, Jan K., "The benefits of codesharing and antitrust immunity for international passengers, with an application to the Star alliance", *Journal of Air Transport Management*, Volume 9 (2003), pp. 83-89.

5   Brueckner, Jan K. and Eric Pels, "European airline mergers, alliance consolidation, and consumer welfare", *Journal of Air Transport Management*, Volume 11 (2005), pp. 27-41.

6   Agusdinata, Buyung and Wouter de Klein, "The dynamics of airline alliances", *Journal of Air Transport Management*, Volume 8 (2002), p. 203.

7   Oum, Tae Hoon, Yu, Chunyan, and Anming Zhang, "Global airline alliances: international regulatory issues", *Journal of Air Transport Management*, Volume 7 (2001), pp. 57-62.

8   Agusdinata, Buyung and Wouter de Klein, "The dynamics of airline alliances", *Journal of Air Transport Management*, Volume 8 (2002), pp. 202 and 203.

9   Kleymann, Birgit and Hannu Seristo, *Managing Strategic Airline Alliances* (Aldershot, UK: Ashgate, 2004), p. x.

10 Segil, Larraine, *Measuring the Value of Partnerships: How to Use Metrics to Plan, Develop, and Implement Successful Alliances* (New York; American Management Association, 2004).

11 Tisch, Jonathan M., *The Power of We: Succeeding Through Partnerships*, (Hoboken, NJ: John Wiley & Sons, 2004).

12 Tisch, Jonathan M., *The Power of We: Succeeding Through Partnerships*, (Hoboken, NJ: John Wiley & Sons, 2004), pp. 3 and 112.

13 Segil, Larraine, *Measuring the Value of Partnerships: How to Use Metrics to Plan, Develop, and Implement Successful Alliances* (New York; American Management Association, 2004), Chapter 11.

14 Segil, Larraine, *Measuring the Value of Partnerships: How to Use Metrics to Plan, Develop, and Implement Successful Alliances* (New York; American Management Association, 2004), pp. 245 and 268.

15 Albers, Sascha, Koch Benjamin, and Christine Ruff, "Strategic alliances between airlines and airports—theoretical assessment and practical evidence", *Journal of Air Transport Management*, Volume 11 (2005), pp. 49-58.

16 For a good description of the negotiating and the governance process and the complexity of the day to day activity, see a quote from a former Northwest executive in Rhoades, Dawna, L., *Evolution of International Aviation: Phoenix Rising* (Aldershot, UK: Ashgate Publishing, 2003), p. 79.

17 Information based on a study by FutureBrand.

18 Nilson Report, Number 807, March 2004. General purpose cards worldwide: Visa, 62%, MasterCard, 32%, American Express, 3%, JCB, 3%, Diners Club, <1%.

Chapter 8

Managing the New Pilots

Throughout this book, we have examined the implications of two conclusions about the airline industry. First, major airlines underestimated the second generation of new airlines who are not just price driven. Consumers embraced their product not so much because it was low priced but more because it provided a better value. Second, based on surveys, consumers rank conventional airlines lower than the new generation unconventional airlines. One clear conclusion then is that the conventional airlines are not delivering value. How do the conventional airlines regain control of their business? Some of the answers lie in:

- Finding more effective ways of communicating with targeted customers about their needs.

- Treating customers as business investments.

- Moving up the "forgetting curve" rather than the "learning curve".

- Trying to stay ahead of the customer.

Communicating with Customers on their Problems

As stated in the first chapter, nowadays passengers not only have greater demands but they also want their demands to be heard. They no longer want to be passive, they want to be active. In other words, they are not satisfied with take it leave it service options and simply receiving one way information from businesses. They would like to have a voice in the nature of products and services they want—price-service options, time of delivery and channels of distribution as well as communication. Businesses say that they do communicate with customers through market research. They claim that after conducting the research, they only put in the marketplace products designed in response to expressed customers needs. For example, a major consideration to the introduction of a simplified fare structure was consumer demand for simpler fares. Yet, many businesses discover that customers are not buying the products, despite being developed based, presumably, on customer feedback.

Although unlikely, could this gap between customer and businesses be due to customers simply not knowing what they want? More likely, the answer, according to some business analysts, is not the lack of initiative to conduct market research to determine customer needs, but the type of market research conducted does not enable consumers to express what they want or businesses to comprehend what they want.[1] Why is market research not producing results that reflect market reality? One main reason could be that senior executives are under pressure to explain what is going on in the marketplace. It is not unheard of to see market research directed more to verify the results expected by the executives and less to determine the true dynamics of the marketplace. Some people would go so far as to say that some executives have used market research to substantiate their already formed positions.[2] It could also be that product life cycles are much shorter due to modern life.

The following section provides a brief summary of the weaknesses of the traditional market research techniques in the current environment and some new channels to communicate with a broader spectrum of consumers in timely and meaningful ways.

Traditional Communication Approaches

Traditionally, businesses dealt with the area of customer insights through focus groups, questionnaires, various forms of Customer Relationship Management (CRM), and mystery shoppers. However, each of these forms of communication has had problems. Consider the weaknesses of just two techniques—focus groups and CRM—not due to any problem with the techniques themselves but mostly to (a) the way the techniques have been used, and (b) their ineffectiveness to address the changing behavior of consumers.

It has already been mentioned that segmentation is a proven business tool that is still relevant—what must change is the interpretation of the results and the recommended actions due to dramatic changes brought about by the consumer movement. Moreover, market research techniques are still valid, but managers must look at results differently, and develop and implement new solutions.

Let us, first, take focus groups.

- Information obtained from a dozen people participating in a focus group does not provide a good representation of the behavior of millions of passengers or, in some cases, the target market segment. Besides the sheer volume of passengers, as shown in Chapter 1, there are dozens of categories and sub-categories of passengers, exemplified by the New Hampshire Netjetter at one end to the Shanghai School Teacher at the other. Each customer behaves differently and has different expectations for different elements of the product. According to many passengers traveling in economy class, airlines spend a disproportionate amount of time looking into the products and services for premium passengers—the lie-flat beds and gourmet meals— at the expense of either the needs of leisure-VFR travelers or the basic product needs of all travelers. How much focus, ask some passengers, should be on glamour and creature comforts for the few and how much on basics for everyone? It is understandable that airlines justify the time and effort on premium passengers because of the disproportionate amount of revenue they provide. However, even that effort may be misguided because no two premium passengers are alike.

- Focus groups are asked specific questions of concern to the airline (relating to, for example, first class seats or kiosks for check-in) and the discussion is often directed in a certain way to get a certain reaction—reactions that may not be of concern to customers. A focus group may, for example, be targeted at extremely specific issues such as the design of a first class seat, or a specific aspect of in-flight entertainment, or the potential use of the Internet. Even when the information sought does relate to product design, it is not sufficiently comprehensive. For example, input is needed not only in the product design but also in the product delivery—such as staffing in reservations, at airports and in flight. How about asking passengers their opinion on tradeoffs, say, between twin aisle aircraft with connecting service vs. nonstop service on a single aisle aircraft, including the possibility of a regional jet? It is important to keep in mind that the large vs. small airplane is a typical operations focused type of question—one would expect a passenger to say bigger is better. Does that really provide meaningful insight into what a passenger will do when it comes time to buy tickets for a business trip or a family vacation? Focus group discussion should emphasize total travel experience— why, where, when, and how do you travel. The interviewer must keep in mind that no one wants to purchase air travel. The question is, what can an airline do to make the travel portion of the trip less onerous?

- Focus groups do not provide information either on a large scale basis or on an individual basis. Based on input from a small sample, marketing departments are forced to make decisions effecting everyone. Even with a large sample, if the correct questions are not asked, marketing departments may end up looking at the data from the wrong perspective. Focus groups are the beginning of research, not the end. They are good for getting reaction to ideas, but not for making go/no-go decisions because the sample sizes are too small. The next step can be surveys and or conjoint analyses to determine whether target markets are interested in various products and how much value they place in each new innovation. Next come techniques, briefly mentioned below, that take us deeper in customer insights.

- Most product changes reflect competitive moves rather than customer input. Even though supported by strong market research supporting the change, recent pricing changes reflect the competitive need to stop or slow the market share shift to unconventional airlines, not to meet the desires of customers who want structural changes to fares.

- In some cases, although communication with customers has been a two way affair, it has been more push information and less pull information. The situation is, in fact, worse, given that customers feel that they have provided information but that management has not listened. For example, for how long have passengers living in reasonable size catchment areas been asking for nonstop service rather than being forced to connect through mega hubs? While airlines may say that going through hubs may result in higher frequency and/or lower fares, it is the customer's voice that should count. It was the entry by unconventional airlines and not the feedback from customers that is finally making conventional airlines sit up and listen to the passengers' desires for better value. When the airline industry was a commodity, innovation did not need to be driven by passengers, it was driven in response to competitive actions. As the airline industry began to lose its commodity status with unconventional airline innovations, commodity industry responses (lowering fares) is no longer working.

- According to some market researchers, focus group participants often receive compensation. Some researchers even go so far as to admit that there are people who are "professional focus group attendees" and who earn their reward by doing and saying what they think the airline wants to hear.

The information obtained through focus groups can be meaningless in today's world in which customers (a) are interested in their total experience, and (b) customers are forming opinions at all touch points, every day and at electronic speeds (given the traditional resources such as radios, televisions, and newspapers, as well as the Internet). Given the widespread customer acceptance of online shopping (whereby key strokes can provide greater insights into customer requests) and advances in data mining algorithms, there is no reason why airlines cannot completely rethink ways to collect and analyze their customers' behaviors.

Next, take briefly the case of CRM. While there is nothing wrong with the concept, the use of the technique has caused problems. For example:

- Some passengers view the technique more as a way for an airline to "send" information, than as a way to "receive" information. The deployment of the technique has added more value for businesses than for passengers. In the case of airlines, for instance, some companies have used CRM to promote their schedules and get passengers to fly more, or to sell excess capacity via promotions, rather than ask about their problems and their experiences. From one perspective, it can be concluded that CRM has been treated as customer information management rather than the often promoted customer relationship management.

- The technique has not been used to seek input from passengers on their concerns with the airline in general or specific areas of service or product features. Even worse, the technique has not been used to seek input on whether an airline can alter its network or schedules to make it easier for passengers to do business with the airline. To some extent, this type of communication does not exist even with the most profitable passengers, let alone the masses. It is a pity since technology exists to have this type of engagement, both on the ground and in flight.[3]

- Think about the information received from airlines with frequent flyer statements. Not only is the information similar to that from other airlines but in many cases of no interest to many recipients. Mileage statements are accompanied by flyers showing "deals" regarding telephone service providers, bank products, hotels and car rentals. Airlines offer free miles to passengers for signing up to take advantage of these deals. Some customers ask: "Why do airlines not use the communication channel for some meaningful and mutually beneficial engagement with passengers?"

- CRM can allow customers to engage not only with management but also employees—especially employees in different functions, not just customer contact employees but also employees performing back office functions. How often do customers get shuffled from one employee to another employee or from one department to another department? CRM can provide the capability for an employee to get for a customer not just any answer but a correct answer.

- Many airlines choose to communicate with passengers based on their frequent flyer mileage status and not on the value of customers. For example, an airline may decide to survey passengers with a certain mileage status. This choice of segmentation for customer feedback is questionable. Did the passenger accumulate 50,000 miles by commuting between two points using the lowest fares, purchasing back-to-back tickets, and purchasing all kinds of products and services having nothing to do with air travel? For example, 15,000 miles for signing up to get a particular credit card coupled with 10,000 miles for signing up to get service with a particular telephone company could qualify the receiver to get a free ticket and receive immediate status in the frequent flyer programs. How does this status qualify the receiver to provide meaningful input on product design or travel experience or management of customer expectations?

New Communication Approaches

From the previous discussion, traditional market research techniques, particularly focus groups, are no longer adequate to determine insight into customers' travel experience, or their attitudes about some aspect such as the airline reward systems. They simply do not raise relevant questions. The need for real customer insight will become more compelling when CEOs start demanding more accountability from marketing (relating to, for example, reasonable ROI on marketing initiatives). Customer insights will become imperative and market research will need to be answering provocative questions like this:

- "How do you shop?" "What services or features that we currently provide would you be willing to give up to have a lower price?"

- "If there are lower base fares, would you be willing to incrementally pay for additional services?"

- "What do you feel is a fair price to pay for a flight between A and B if it included or did not include food (cold but of reasonable quality), assigned seating and fast check-in with no hassles?"

- "How do you feel about our business class cabin configuration on long haul flights, for example, about having a middle seat in a business class cabin?"

- "Are you satisfied with our loyalty program? For example, how satisfied are you with our upgrade system, especially now that load factors are running very high and upgrades can be purchased by anyone for 50-100 dollars?"

- "How should we communicate with you to tell you what we have done about your suggestions?"

- "Can you tell us more about your travel behavior? We only partially know you based on your actual transaction history— the times you traveled, the fares you paid and the classes of service you booked."

- "What do you think are our strengths and weaknesses (relative to our competitors) in such areas as network, price, and customer service? What would you want in a service?"

- "What in your experience truly differentiates one airline from another?"

Whereas the above examples are too specific and operationally focused, it is also appropriate to ask more basic, open-ended questions. What can we do to make us your airline of choice? What are you most unhappy about when traveling by air? If you ran the airline, what would you do differently? Are you the type of customer who is loyal to a brand or one who always buys the lowest price? How do you define value?

Technology now exists (web-based and with a voice-to-data conversion capability) to handle not only hundreds of thousands of free-form comments based on the aforementioned type of questions but to turn the answers into quantifiable information that can then be used in business design decisions and formulation of customer strategy. Airlines have rarely asked their passengers, by segment, about the issues that affect them. Had airlines been able to ask their profitable passengers questions that provided insight into their attitudes, some of the conventional airlines may not have evolved into "everything to everybody" that satisfy few and may also have slowed the incursions made by unconventional airlines. Continued blindness to the needs of our new pilots can only lead to worse scenarios.

The key elements of the new form of communications are (a) to involve customers on a large scale basis, (b) to engage with customers on a real time basis, where possible, and (c) segment the customers and listen to their concerns from their perspective. This approach to communication with customers is possible, evidenced by the experience of some other leading businesses, and the following developments. First, technology can now address huge volumes of customers. Second, in some parts of the world, the capability now exists to segment the market down to the household income level. Third, the same technology can be used to listen to employees. The pressure by management to reduce costs has increased stress on the front-line staff. Is that not the very last place to compromise the quality of the airline's customer contact personnel? Therefore management also needs to listen to employees and their opinions and experience. Understanding employee attitudes and opinions can assist management to ascertain not only the employees' views of customers' experience but also their views of management policy. The employee is often the first and last point of contact with the customer and it is imperative that the policies and procedures implemented across the business match or enhance the employee capability to represent the airline.

Specifically, airlines can use websites to gather insight into passenger attitudes and opinions and to view their products from the passenger perspective. In response to customer comments, airlines could inform their passengers what it is doing with future products as a result of the passenger' insights. An airline could also explain when and why it cannot act on some passenger suggestions. Would not this form of communications create greater loyalty and in turn positive word-of-mouth advocacy of the airline and its products? The need for customer engagement on a large scale basis is even more critical for the sale of premium products. A good example of this form of customer engagement is General Motors' Vice Chairman, Bob Lutz's web page (GM FastLane Blog) where he talks about issues facing the company and where consumers can post questions that are answered.

The other point mentioned above related to positive word-of-mouth advocacy. Recent research shows that the answer to the following simple question, "Would you recommend this company to a friend or colleague?", may be a better predictor of customer loyalty (and company growth) than other complex customer satisfaction surveys. According to Frederick Reichheld, an excellent way to profitable growth may lie in a company's ability to get its loyal customers to become its marketing department. His research shows remarkable positive correlation within the airline industry between the three year growth (1999-2002) and net promoters (the percentage of customers who are promoters of a brand or company minus the percentage who are detractors).[4] The key to loyalty is to convert customers into promoters.

It is also critical to keep the passenger engaged through the entire travel phase to understand what emotional drivers the passenger is willing to impart. Interactive access to individual seats can allow airlines to engage with passengers in-flight. Cabin crews can be given the tools to capture employee and passenger insight throughout the flight through hand held and/or wireless devices. Direct communications between customer support personnel and in-flight crew may enhance the passenger experience particularly during irregular operations. However, extreme care is needed in this area. While it is desirable to get immediate passenger feedback during the trip, how much can an airline intrude into a traveler's time?

In summary, while traditional approaches to market research—focus groups, surveys and mystery shoppers—do have some value for some businesses, the airline industry needs more sophisticated techniques to communicate with customers and employees. Besides the web-based technology, there are numerous other techniques that can provide useful customer insights. Examples can be found in numerous books.[5]

Managing Customers as Investments

To state that customers are important or that they are assets is hardly a new idea. Businesses know that and have attempted to design their products and services to meet the needs of their customers profitably. However, something must be wrong if the customers are not happy and the company is not making any money. Has the business selected the wrong segment of customers? Has it developed the wrong products and services? Does it need to charge more than the customer is willing to pay? In other words, has the business made poor or incorrect investments in its business design?

More and more business analysts are suggesting that customers should be treated and managed as investments, in that companies should not spend more money on their customers than the customers are worth. In other words, a company should make a business case for its customers just as it does for any other asset. Estimate the current and future costs, the revenue, and the return on investments. Consequently, while neither concept is new—the importance of customers or the development of a business case—what is new is the application of the business case approach to the management of customers as investments. Some business writers have extended their analysis by using the estimated current and future values of customers as a proxy to predict the value of the firm.[6]

The business case approach to customer management is particularly useful for the following reasons.

- It helps to answer the question of the appropriateness of the targeted segment(s), deterring management from falling into the one-size-fits-all approach trap.

- It discourages management from business decisions based simply on metrics such as market share and customer satisfaction. A smaller percentage of high value customers may or may not be worth more than a large percentage of low value customers. Negative value customers need to be discovered and discarded. Southwest chooses not to serve some customers. Why does a major airline feel the need to serve everyone? This type of analysis would also provide the basis for divesting unnecessary resources that today are serving market segments that an airline should abandon. Investment in serving a particular customer segment must show a reasonable return. The approach helps to quantify the relationship between the value a company provides to a customer and the value of that customer to the company— mutual benefit. Management also receives information on (a) which customers' feedback is important, and (b) which customers should get special treatment such as "courtesy" upgrades and special services during irregular operation situations.

- It forces management to compute profitability at a perceptible level—not at aggregated measures such as region, route, product line, fleet, and so forth. One can easily plot a curve, as shown in Figure 8.1, to determine the distribution of passengers by their profitability. This would then be the starting point to determine the strategies to manage customers as investments.

- It forces the development of an analysis to estimate the cost of customer acquisition and customer retention. Again, the concept portrayed in Figure 8.1 shows that businesses should neither allocate investment as a fixed amount per customer, nor as a constant change by value. Rather, the investment decision should be based on the standard financial type of analysis—earnings and cash flow with adjustments for risks such as customer defection. Total investment does not need to increase. The business can spend less on some customers and more on others.

- The analysis can provide insightful information on customer trends. For example, while the cash flow may appear to be constant over the next five years, it may be hiding the fact that an increase in revenue from customer growth may be offset by a decrease in margin due to an increase in competition.

- The approach provides management with some insights into key drivers of customer value—particularly customer life time value. Examine the concept shown in Figure 8.2. Sophisticated airlines have already developed ways of computing the past and future values of customers. For example, examine customers whose expenditures on air travel increased as they rose in their professions. Having reached the peak, the expenditures begin to decline as customers approach their retirement stage. It is possible, however, to gain additional potential value by developing new products for customers by their career stage.

- It also helps to revitalize important customers. Employees would then have a logical explanation as to why they should help and work with a high value but difficult customer.

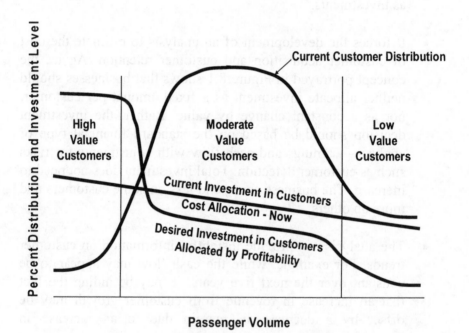

Figure 8.1 Investment Criteria in Customers by Value
Source: Based on Brendan Hickman (Teradata), Presentation made at The Ohio State University and Air India 11th International Airline Symposium, March 21-24, 2004, Cochin, Kerala, India.

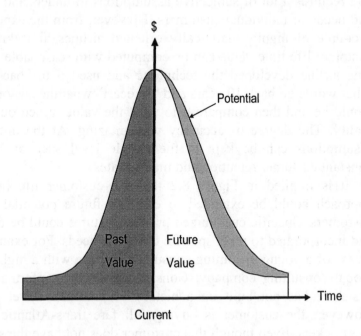

Figure 8.2 Current, Future and Potential Value of Customers

The actual technique for computing the life time value of a customer is based on the standard discounted cash flow model that starts with an initial investment required for the acquisition of a customer and the cash flows generated by the customer over the customer's life time. Input is needed on factors such as the customer defection rate, the variation in product purchases and product margins, customer life span, and costs of customer acquisition and retention.[7] Based on some real case studies within the airline industry, two other important factors have emerged for computing the life time value of customers: (a) customers' buying criteria, and (b) the use of a weighting scheme in computing the current value of a customer, with higher weights assigned to recent purchases.

There is no question that the analysis is extremely data intensive and requires a lot of subjective assumptions to understand the value and needs of individual customers. However, from the experience of a couple of highly analytically oriented airlines, it is known that customer life time value can be computed with reasonable accuracy. One airline developed the technique and used it to "backcast", in other words go back 10 years and "forecast" what the customer value would be and then compare it to what the value turned out to be in reality. The degree of accuracy was amazing. At the initial stage, assumptions can be kept at the simple level such as a relative constant customer retention and margin rates.

It is implied in Figure 8.2 that the customer life time value approach could be extended to estimate future potential value of customers. Specific customized product features could be developed and incorporated to meet specific customer needs. For example, take a case of a young upcoming consultant starting with a high powered global consulting company. Consider the known information. The customer has not built up a history of premium travel purchase. However, the customer is buying full fare trans-Atlantic business class tickets. Even though this customer does not have the status in a frequent flyer program to be upgraded immediately to the higher cabin, should the airline upgrade this customer or another one who has the status in the mileage category but is about to retire from the same company? For the young traveler, an upgrade to first class while on business as well as an upgrade to business class while on a personal trip, would buy a lot of brand loyalty and enhance customer life time value. Such strategic applications enable an airline to make investments in a future frequent flyer.

This type of analysis fits right in with the customer-driven business strategy discussed in other chapters such as business designs, in Chapter 3, and product renovation and innovation, in Chapter 4. Moreover, it forces management to examine its marketing decision in every area. Consider the area of branding. If the information revolution is enabling companies to disaggregate its customers and pursue direct marketing, or information-based one-to-one marketing, then is there a need for branding? Branding still has a role; but that role has changed.[8]

Moving Up the Forgetting Curve

The dynamics of the airline industry are changing so rapidly that it is no longer sufficient to develop strategies to survive or even to win: rather, strategies are needed to capture the mindset of our current and future customers. As mentioned before consumers now not only have choice but that choice is spreading. Compare, according to one research study, the availability of choice between the early 1970s and the late 1990s: PC models, zero vs. 400; SUV styles, 8 vs. 38; websites, zero vs. 4,700,000; TV channels in Houston, 5 vs. 185; and McDonald's menu items, 13 vs. 43.[9] The choice in airline service is also increasing although not at the same speed as the choice in some other industries. Consequently, strategies are now needed, according to one expert on strategy, to win the war on customer satisfaction.[10] Given that the dramatic change is not only in consumer behavior and decision making criteria but also in the brutal nature of competition, the "right strategy" may not be the "traditional strategy". Consequently, winning the new war may call for not moving up the "learning curve", but rather moving up the "forgetting curve". Here are some examples of the areas we need to forget.

- Obsession with market share (instead of profit).

- Trying to be all things to all people.

- Trying to serve all markets.

- Believing that it is not possible to "shrink" to profitability.

- Believing that passengers will pay a significant premium for travel on conventional airlines.

- Trying to spend most of the time exploring the needs of premium class passengers and very little time on the needs of economy class passengers (which is the growing segment).

- Focusing on the size of the airline rather than the level of profitability.

- Focusing on an individual airline's own brand without similar focus on the brand of the alliance.

- Holding back on outsourcing many functions because they are considered to be core functions.

- Believing that unconventional airlines cannot compete effectively in certain niches, such as US transcontinental or intercontinental markets.

Conventional strategy is obviously not working. For example, as already mentioned, traditional airlines were quite successful in competing with the first generation of new entrants by matching fares (using sophisticated revenue management systems), dumping capacity and exploiting the brand name. This strategy is not viable today. It does not reflect reality. Consider the fate of businesses that did not face reality—airlines or others—that kept their focus on conventional wisdom (TWA, Swissair, AT&T and Lucent, for example).

The key to outperforming competition is to drive change by appreciating and facing the reality of the marketplace. This may require the re-examination of the laws of supply and demand. We need to not only understand the characteristics of the current demand, but also to predict the emerging needs of our targeted markets, and to develop products that best meet the genuine needs of the targeted customers, rather than compete on price.[11] Price isn't everything. In order to predict the trends consumers are likely to embrace and the potential disruptive strategies of the next generation of competitors, we need to see things differently and question the routine.[12] Businesses also need to decide whether they want to be "customer pleasers or efficiency crunchers".[13] Finally, to succeed in the fiercely competitive environment, the appropriate strategy may well be to make competition irrelevant by moving to an uncontested market space.[14] For example, there are dozens of entrepreneurs planning to start low-cost, low fare airlines in the already congested US domestic market—"the red ocean strategy". There are two that are exploring plans to develop service in uncontested market space (on-demand air taxi service[15])—"blue ocean strategy".[16] The formulation of strategies within this type of a framework would require moving up the forgetting curve—letting go of the old and getting hold of the new.

Flying Ahead of the Customer

What are the implications for airline management of the statement "good pilots fly ahead of their planes"? Two possibilities exist. First, they need to achieve deep customer focus.[17] This includes not only an understanding of the mindset of the current customers today and in the future but also what will be the mindset of future customers—for example, the "computer game generation".[18] Second, they need to understand not only what kind of innovations could dramatically reshape the aviation industry but also the full spectrum of competitive strategies of current and future unconventional airlines.

Relating to the first point, if the conventional airlines missed the needs of the passengers who diverted to unconventional airlines (because of better value, not just lower price), then what do we know about the needs of next generation of customers? Going back to the computer game generation for a minute, according to researchers, not only will this generation dominate the workforce, but their dramatically different attitudes, expectations and abilities are already changing the rules of the business.[19]

Relating to the second point, what happens when (not if) aircraft manufacturers introduce "game changing" airplanes? Following are just two examples. What would be the impact of a totally new 100-seat aircraft with the unit operating costs of a 200 seat wide body aircraft, trans-Atlantic range, and reasonable passenger appeal (relating, for example, to cabin configuration and in-flight entertainment and services—power points for laptops and access to Internet)? What would be the impact of very light jets (3-4 seats) that are now being explored for safe and economical on-demand taxi services in short haul markets? The availability of viable technology—both aircraft and online distribution—can now make it possible for passengers to make day trips, paying approximately the equivalent of current airline full fares.[20] In one way, saving on hotel and meal expenses by returning home the same day would push the total cost down below the equivalent airline full fare. As to the potential strategies of current and new unconventional airlines, the range goes from those who offer bare-bone services at the lowest price, to those who offer similar products but at lower prices, to those who offer a better product at the same price, to those who offer much superior product at slightly higher prices.[21]

From this perspective, it is not just the conventional airlines but also the unconventional airlines that must rely on the use of innovation theories to spot industry transforming businesses and business models.[22] Can passengers be processed at airports for air travel similar to the way they are processed at railway stations for travel on trains? Which aspects of the business model of Federal Express can be applied to the transportation of passengers?

Closing Thoughts

We are seeing a fundamental change in consumer behavior, consumer demographics, as well as high risk and paradigm breaking technology (ranging from telecommunications, to information, to aircraft). This change is necessitating comprehensive consumer insights to develop end-to-end roadmaps of product designs and customer experience. If indeed the passenger is now flying the plane, then to regain control of the business, airline management must, with both feet clearly planted in marketplace realities, drive change to unlock new sources of profitability. Managements must not only think boldly but also execute courageously and relentlessly ground-breaking and business-altering initiatives to keep their airlines fiercely competitive and fly ahead of their customers. Although the first phase of the process is still the old concept of segmenting, targeting, and positioning, what is new is:

- Interpreting the results differently.

- Asking smart questions and getting the right facts.

- Changing from inside-out to outside-in thinking.

- Doing a cost-benefit analysis on solutions for customers.

- Co-creating value through constant customer engagement.

- Seeing the forest and the trees.

- Being prepared for surprises.

- Accepting uncomfortable answers.

- Partnering within the value chain.

- Avoiding the herd mentality.

- Combating the transitional issues, and last but not least.

- Challenging the relevance of entrenched mindsets about critical success factors in the emerging marketplace.

The above points may seem to be academic but they do apply to a number of cases within the airline industry. Here are just three examples. First, management at some airlines continue to think from the inside-out perspective rather than the outside-in perspective. Alliances tend to be established much more to meet some needs of an airline rather than the passenger. Is an airline willing to accept an uncomfortable answer of letting go of 40 percent of its frequent flyer passengers on whom the airline is losing money? In the US, is one of the major airlines willing to outsource most of its domestic capacity and focus strictly on international services, thereby reducing its size by 50 percent? How many airlines are willing to combat the transitional issues and to take substantial losses in the short time to dramatically realign their fleet for the long term?

Once the segmenting, targeting, and positioning decision has been made, management must then inextricably link corporate strategies, culture and organizational structures to persuade their targeted customers of the value of their unique and differentiated value propositions. Again, there is clear evidence of the lack of this linkage at many conventional airlines but it does exist at some of the unconventional airlines such as jetBlue that appears to have aligned its' organization's skills, resources and culture around its targeted segment of customers. Finally, there must be clear and meaningful incentives and controls relating to the execution of strategy, whether it is as basic as improving on-time performance or as complex as making domestic and cross border mergers and acquisitions work to move the airline business ahead.

Notes

[1] Zaltman, Gerald, *How Customers Think: Essential Insights into the Mind of the Market* (Boston: MA: Harvard University Press, 2003).

[2] Barwise, Patrick and Sean Meehan, *simply Better: Winning and Keeping Customers by Delivering What Matters Most* (Boston: Harvard University Press, 2004), p. 154.

[3] Information based on communications with Robert Trevelyan of Trevelyan Associates during February and March of 2005.

[4] Reichheld, Frederick F., "The One Number You Need to Grow", *Harvard Business Review*, December 2003, pp. 46-54.

[5] Kotler, Philip, *Ten Deadly Marketing Sins: Signs and Solutions* (Hoboken, NJ: John Wiley & Sons, 2004).

[6] Gupta, Sunil and Donald R. Lehmann, *Managing Customers as Investments: The Strategic Value of Customers in the Long Run* (Upper Saddle River, NJ: Wharton School Publishing, 2005).

[7] Gupta, Sunil and Donald R. Lehmann, *Managing Customers as Investments: The Strategic Value of Customers in the Long Run* (Upper Saddle River, NJ: Wharton School Publishing, 2005), Appendices A-C.

[8] Dewar, Niraj, "What Are Brands Good For?", *MIT Sloan Management Review*, Fall 2004, pp. 31-37.

9   Trout, Jack, *Trout on Strategy: Capturing Mindshare, Conquering Markets* (New York: McGraw-Hill, 2004), p. 7.

10 Trout, Jack, *Trout on Strategy: Capturing Mindshare, Conquering Markets* (New York: McGraw-Hill, 2004), p. 37.

11 Kash, Rick, *The New Law of Supply and Demand: he Revolutionary New Demand Strategy for Faster Growth and Higher Profits* (New York: Currency and Doubleday, 2001).

12 Wind, Yoram (Jerry) and Colin Crook, *The Power of Impossible Thinking: Transform the Business of Your Life and the Life of Your Business* (Upper Saddle River, NJ: Wharton School Publishing, 2005), pp. 84-86, 236, 251.

13 Arussy, Lior, *Passionate Profitable: Why Customer Strategies Fail and 10 Steps to do them Right* (Hoboken, NJ: John Wiley & Sons, 2005).

14 Kim, W. Chan and Renée Mauborgne, *Blue Ocean Strategy: How to Create Uncontested Market Space and Make the Competition Irrelevant* (Boston, MA: Harvard Business School Press, 2005).

15 Lunsford, Lynn, "Air-Taxi Venture Set to Start Service in Mid-2006", *Wall Street Journal*, April 25, 2005, p. B4.

16 Kim, W. Chan and Renée Mauborgne, "Blue Ocean Strategy", *Harvard Business Review*, October 2004, pp. 76-84.

17 Vandermerwe, Sandra, "Achieving Deep Customer Focus", *MIT Sloan Management Review*, Spring 2004, pp. 26-34.

18 These are people who play digital games. One group of researchers show that the gamer generation is already bigger than the baby boom and will have a profound impact on the future of business. See, Beck, John C. and Mitchell Wade, *Got Game: How the Gamer Generation is Reshaping Business Forever* (Boston, MA: Harvard Business School Press, 2004).

19 Beck, John C. and Mitchell Wade, *Got Game: How the Gamer Generation is Reshaping Business Forever* (Boston, MA: Harvard Business School Press, 2004), jacket text.

20 Lunsford, Lynn, "Air-Taxi Venture Set to Start Service in Mid-2006", *Wall Street Journal*, April 25, 2005, p. B4.

21 Potter, Don, "Confronting Low-End Competition", *MIT Sloan Management Review*, Summer 2004, pp. 73-78.

22 For an insightful discussion on this topic, see, Christensen, Clayton M., Anthony, Scott D. and Erik A. Roth, *Seeing What's Next: Using the Theories on Innovation to Predict Industry Change* (Boston, MA: Harvard Business School Press, 2004).

Index

About the Author

Nawal Taneja has more than 30 years of experience in the airline industry. As a practitioner, he has worked for and advised major airlines and airline-related businesses worldwide in the areas of strategic and tactical planning. His experience also includes the presidency of a small airline that provided scheduled and charter service with jet aircraft, and the presidency of a research organization that provided consulting services to the air transportation community worldwide. In academia, he has served as Professor and Chairman of the Aerospace Engineering and Aviation Department at the Ohio State University, and has served as an Associate Professor in the Flight Transportation Laboratory of the Department of Aeronautics and Astronautics of the Massachusetts Institute of Technology. On the government side, he has advised civil aviation authorities in public policy areas such as airline liberalization, air transportation bilateral and multilateral agreements, and the management and operations of government-owned airlines. He has also served on the board of public and private organizations.

Nawal Taneja recently authored three books for practitioners in the airline industry: (1) *Driving Airline Business Strategies through Emerging Technology* published in 2002; (2) *Airline Survival Kit: Breaking Out of the Zero Profit Game* published in 2003; and (3) *Simpli-Flying: Optimizing the Airline Business Model* published in 2004. All three books were published by the Ashgate Publishing Company.